A Wesley Family Book of Days

A Wesley Family Book of Days

Compiled and Edited by
Susan Pellowe

Renard Productions
Aurora, Illinois

Edinburgh

Newcastle

Epworth

Manchester

London

Bristol

Cape
Cornwall

Scilly Isles

A Wesley Family Book of Days
Compiled and Edited by Susan Pellowe
©1994 Susan Pellowe

ISBN 0-9623507-1-0
Library of Congress Catalog Card Number: 94-68425
First Edition

Printed by River Street Press, Aurora, Illinois USA

The window on the cover is a window in the birthplace of
Susanna Annesley Wesley, Spital Yard, London.

Cover design by David Renar

DEDICATION

For the Pellowe family,
whose support is endless,
and for my extended family,
whose curiosity caused this book.

Or, in the words of John Wesley—

To my relations

*To all that are endeared to me by
their kindnesses or acquaintance*

*To all who remember me in their prayers
or desire to be remembered in mine.*

PRELUDE

This *Wesley Family Book of Days* has come into being because I could not find anything like it. As I travel about performing Susanna Wesley, I find people curious to learn more in a casual way and eager for a casual book. This book is for them.

When people move, in our age of ecumenism and transcience, they join a compatible local congregation. Comfort level with the style of worship and liturgy, agreement with social mission, convenience of transportation and hours of worship tend to be far more influential than denominational history or theology. I know one family in England that chose a church because it had reliable heating! For such members, the heritage of belief is at best icing on the cake. Perhaps rightfully so. Beyond these temporal considerations, they seek God, Christ, and the Holy Spirit, not Luther, Knox, Wesley or Fox.

But the icing on the cake adds flavor and enriches the cake. The icing is fun. Everyone wants at least a fingerful. And so we return to why I have compiled this glimpse into the Wesley family.

Family experiences flavored this denomination called Methodist. The Wesleys struggled with poverty and the father went to prison because he could not pay his debts; their house burned to the ground, leaving them homeless and the family fragmented; lack of good local schools meant that the mother educated them at home; adults suffered serious illnesses and infant mortality rate was high. (Does any of this sound familiar?) Brothers John and Charles Wesley visited prisons, gave money and shelter to those in need, founded schools and encouraged study, opened a free clinic, and John wrote a best-selling medical guide called *Primitive Physic*. The parents lived by a schedule in order to get the most out of every day; the boys copied that method and, in an age of loose social codes, earned the misunderstanding of thousands and the derisive nickname of "Method-ists". They persevered in the name of Christ and changed at least one nation.

Were they stuffy, pious work-aholics? Read between the lines: "Help me to overcome habitual levity in my thoughts," wrote Susanna. Doesn't that sound as though she can't help harboring some light moments? A man comes to hear John Wesley, his pockets full of old eggs which get squashed in his pockets and Wesley writes "in an instant he was perfume." John Wesley is one of the best travelled, best-read men in the country with a wealth of anecdotes and Christian cheer that make him a coveted houseguest.

A Wesley Family Book of Days makes no attempt to lay out the entire family history nor the organization of the Methodist Societies, as they were called, nor to follow the argument of whether those societies should separate from the Church of England in which its founders lived and died as ordained priests. It is rather my personal collection of some favorite passages from Wesley writings, together with a few key events in the lives of the family and the reluctant forming of a new denomination.

One cannot consider the Wesleys without considering Christianity and particularly Methodism. Prayers, spiritual ponderings, and definitions of basic Wesley terms occupy a number of days. The family was close knit, but it had what we now call its dysfunctional bits. Some of these are here, too. Why? Because I think it helps to know that those advising us or looking like examples from history's pages have, like us, struggled with loss, disappointment, and even unbelief. What use could they be to us otherwise?

Browse. Heap your spoon with icing. If you insist on more cake, refer to the bibliography. Sing the songs. Weep for the sad days, cherish the good ones, share them all. "You cannot be warm alone...."

Susan Pellowe
Chicago, 1994

Acknowledgments

Books do not happen without dozens of people befriending the author. Each brings a unique expertise or access to material; each contributes a special piece of lifeline to the final creation. I am aware that many of the people listed here have silent assistants next to them, and my gratitude extends to those helpers as well.
Thank You to...

Joyce Banks, Librarian of the Wesley Historical Society Library at Westminster College, Oxford, who sent packets of material exceeding my hopes; some of the items look dangerously like the beginnings of another project

Colin Barton, Warden of The Old Rectory, Epworth, for information, references, and photos

A.M. Bishop, School Archivist at Kingswood School, Bath, for his thorough response

Myra Burge and Jackie Ruhl for laughter and faith at the midnight hour

Richard Douglas, artist, and friend of the Old Rectory in Epworth, whose generosity with his own art and with Methodist art in his collection greatly enriches these pages

Peter S. Forsaith, who is the proverbial fountain of knowledge about Methodist-related art, and who has been incredibly thoughtful as he shares that, even in the midst of completing his own book on John Fletcher of Madeley

Joy Fox, Archivist at the Methodist Church Overseas Division in London, whose timing brightened grey Chicago days with stunning photos of art work held at her offices

Lawrence Gunn, who in the midst of leaving his post as Custodian of Bristol New Room, most carefully superintended the completion of my requests

Rev. Seymour Halford, my pastor, whose encouragement takes the form of useful brainstorming, names and addresses, and peace, grace, and humor

David Himrod, Head Librarian at Garrett Evangelical Theological Seminary in Evanston, Illinois, for being that marvelous thing, a cheerful and resourceful librarian

Daniel Lang, President of River Street Press, whose own Christian commitment makes him a joy to work with; and his dedicated staff, whose extra efforts improved the product

Rev. Tim S. Macquiban of the Archives and History Committee of The Methodist Church in Britain and of the Wesley Historical Society, for his recommendation for permission to reproduce material and for forwarding my requests to such reliable, knowledgeable researchers

Rev. James R. McGraw, Pastor of Old John Street United Methodist Church in New York, for help with the Charterhouse portrait of John Wesley

Geoffrey E. Milburn of Sutherland, for his enormous generosity with materials and information at the eleventh hour

Rev. Peter B. Mortlock and **Rev. David Urquhart** of Coventry, and **Richard Bowden-Dan** of London, for taking time to run down dead ends for me—which are every bit as important as fertile pathways—and for writing good-naturedly about them

Mary Lou Perkins, proofreader and editorial sounding board, who went the second mile

Rohan Quine, Photo Librarian of the British Tourist Authority in New York, who understood the need to dig beyond tourist photos and put me in touch with archival documentation; and to tourist centers and museums at Spalding and the National Trust at Wicken Fen.

David Renar, photographer and designer, whose playfulness and expertise with computer photos and whose advice have greatly enhanced many of the images in this book

The John Rylands University Library of Manchester: to **J.P.Tuck,** Head of Administration, and to **Mr. Gareth Lloyd,** Archivist of the Methodist Church Archives housed there for permission to quote and reproduce as indicated in the bibliography; to their staff for extraordinary assistance in helping to make the most of my brief time in their reading room; and a special debt of gratitude to **Dr. Peter Nockles** of the Methodist Archives for his attentiveness and his prompt progress reports across the Atlantic

Service Corps of Retired Executives in Chicago, specifically **Abraham Lecker** and **Norbert J. Sweete,** who helped more than they know to launch the project in this format

David Siegfried, for SOS computer expertise and design assistance

Alison Taylor, Curator of the Museum of Methodism at City Road in London, for being a touchstone! Her rapport with material and keepers of material, her fax-ability, her willingness to let me tap her brain and resources, her tolerance of endless requests, and as much as anything her enthusiasm for the project have been, in a word, invaluable.

Brian Taylor, Secretary of the North East Wesley Historical Society, for expediting response to a call for help

Mark Trewin and Wendy Trewin, who made the gathering of photos and material in London for me a family project

Rev. Dr. R. John Tudor, Superintendent Minister of Westminster Central Hall London, for his abounding humor, his love of Jesus Christ, and his sense of Methodist history; his questions about Susanna Wesley and her family unfailingly produce inspiration and more research.

Trustees, Custodians, Wardens, and Committees of Bristol New Room, Epworth Old Rectory, John Rylands University Library Manchester, Methodist Church Overseas Division, The Museum of Methodism, Wesley's City Road Chapel, World Methodist Council, and the Wesley Historical Society for ready permissions to use material in their keeping.

THE FAMILY
Branches of the family tree included in
A Wesley Family Book of Days

Susanna Annesley Wesley 1669 - 1742

Maternal Grandfather: John White, a Welsh Puritan, distinguished lawyer, and Member of Parliament from Southwark. He was nicknamed "Century White" because he exposed the immorality of 100 clergy.

Mother (name unknown)

Paternal Grandparents: Rev. John Anslye and Judith. John Anslye died when their son Samuel was four years old, leaving Mrs. Anslye to raise him alone.

Father: Rev. Samuel Annesley (1620-1696), only son and named after the prophet, was dedicated at birth "for the work of the ministry." From the age of six he read twenty chapters of the Bible daily. He was a highly respected and much loved preacher, pastor, and writer. Although his background was Puritan and Presbyterian, his licensing came through the Church of England. As a matter of conscience, he refused to sign the Act of Uniformity agreeing to changes in the Church of England Prayer Book, so in 1662 he preached his last sermon as Vicar of St. Giles Cripplegate. Rev. Annesley founded a new congregation at St. Helen's, Bishopsgate, in Spital Yard. He married twice. There were 25 children. Tradition says 24 of them were by Susanna's mother.

Of the 24 **siblings of Susanna Annesley** we know the names of **Elizabeth, Judith, Anne, and Sarah**; and one brother, **Samuel** (c. 1658-1732). Brother **Samuel** apparently made money while in India and indicated he would help the Wesleys. Susanna traveled to London to meet him on his return, but he never arrived. An unsolved mystery, his disappearance is credited to foul play. **Elizabeth** left some writings that indicate her to be of the same spiritual nature as Susanna; it was said that to know one was to know the other.

Judith married **John Dunton**, a London bookseller and free spirit, who published Samuel Wesley's first book and was a partner in producing a serial, *The Athenian Gazette*. **Susanna** at the time of her confirmation, despite her father's dissent against the Church of England, chose to join that church. Her strong heritage of Puritanism and reasoned dissent, combined with wholehearted devotion to the Anglican church, were major influences on her children and, hence, on Methodism.

Samuel Wesley 1662 - 1735

Maternal Grandfather: Rev. John White of Dorchester

Mother (name unknown): niece of Rev. Dr. Thomas Fuller, chaplain to King Charles II

Paternal Grandfather: Bartholomew Wesley, born 1599; educated at Oxford in medicine and theology. He is said to have died brokenhearted because of the persecution of his son.

Father: Rev. John Westley. Oxford graduate, with a degree in Oriental studies. He had the living of Winterborn-Whitchurch. He was a Dissenter during the Restoration, however, which relegated him to poverty. In defiance of the Five Miles Act of 1665, he preached near former churches. For these acts of protest and conscience, John Westley was imprisoned four times and tormented, leading to his early death. He is buried in the churchyard at Preston "in an undistinguished grave." Rev. Wesley's wife struggled to give her sons good educations.

Four **siblings: Timothy; Matthew,** an apothecary and surgeon in London, who was very generous to Samuel's children by bringing different ones to London to live with him both after the 1709 fire and later; **Elizabeth**; and **Rev. Samuel Wesley**. Samuel, although the son of a Dissenter and schooled in their academies, chose to join the Church of England, which enabled him to attend Oxford. He later wrote against dissenters.

The Family

Samuel Wesley and Susanna Annesley

Married in London November 12, 1688, they lived first in Holborn. Rev. Wesley served briefly as curate at St. Botolph's, Aldersgate, then as a chaplain on a man-o'-war. In 1691 he accepted the post of chaplain to the Marquis of Normanby and the family moved to South Ormsby. In 1697(?) they moved to Epworth, where Rev. Wesley was rector of St. Andrew's Parish Church until his death in 1735. In 1724 the living of Wroote, five miles from Epworth, was added to Rev. Wesley's curacy. He arranged for the Wroote living to pass to Rev. John Whitelamb upon the marriage of Whitelamb to Molly Wesley. Susanna and Samuel Wesley had 19 children, ten of whom survived to adulthood.

1. **Samuel, Jr. (Sammy) 1690-1739;** married Ursula Berry in 1715; two children: son Samuel, who died in his teens; and a daughter nicknamed "Phil". Four others died in infancy and are buried in the cloisters of Westminster Abbey. Samuel Wesley, Jr., was a highly respected teacher at Westminster School in London, then Headmaster of Blundell School, the Free Grammar School, in Tiverton.
2. **Susanna** 1691-1693
3. **Emilia (Emily)** 1692-1771; married Robert Harper, an itinerant apothecary, 1735; one daughter, who died in infancy or youth. Robert Harper died 1740.
4. **Annesley** and
5. **Jedediah,** twins 1694-1695; Annesley lived 2 months, Jedediah lived 14 months.
6. **Susanna (Sukey)** 1695-1764; married Richard Ellison; children John, Ann, Deborah, Richard.
7. **Mary (Molly)** 1696-1734; married Rev. John Whitelamb (1710-1769) December 21, 1733; died in childbirth with first child, who also died.
8. **Mehetabel (Hetty)** 1697-1750; married William Wright, October 13, 1725. All children died at birth or soon after.
9. **Infant,** sex not known 1698: soon died.
10. **John** 1699: soon died.
11. **Benjamin** 1700: soon died.
12. **Unnamed twin** 1701: soon died.
13. **Unnamed twin** 1701: soon died.
14. **Anne (Nancy)** 1702-?; married John Lambert December 2, 1725. One son, John, born 1726.

The Family

15. **John (Jack)** 1703-1791; married Mrs. Mary Vazeille, widow of a well-to-do merchant. No children, although she had four by her first marriage.
16. **Son** accidentally smothered by nurse 1705, age three weeks.
17. **Martha (Patty)** 1706-1791; married Westley Hall September 13, 1735; they had ten children; one son lived to the age of 14; the rest died in infancy.
18. **Charles** 1707-1788
    Married Sarah Gwynne (**Sally**) 1726-1822; eight children, three of whom survived infancy. Baptismal entry of first child in register of St. James's Church, Bristol, reads "John Wesley, of Charles and of Sarah a Precher in the Horsfaier."
    1. **John (Jacky)** 1752, died at 16 months.
    2. **Martha Maria** 1755, died when a month old.
    3. **Charles** 1757-1834, became a well-known organist; never married.
    4. **Sarah (Sally)** 1759 - 1828; wrote some and kept house for brother Charles; never married.
    5. **Susanna** 1761, died age 11 months.
    6. **Selina** 1764, died age 5 weeks.
    7. **Samuel** 1766-1837, became a noted composer and musician. His father on his own deathbed said, "I shall have to bless God through all eternity that ever you were born. We shall meet in heaven."
    8. **John James** 1768, died age 7 months.
19. **Kezziah (Kezzy)** 1709-1741; never married.

The eminent Methodist historian Frank Baker believes that references in Wesley family correspondence indicate a different birth order than had been traditionally listed. In *Methodist History* for April 1988, he presents this sequence, beginning after Mehetabel:

    9: Unknown sex, 1698
    10 and 11: John and Benjamin, May 16, 1699; die 1700
    12 and 13: John Benjamin and Anne, May 17, 1701;
       John Benjamin dies December 30, 1701
    14: John, June 17, 1703
    15: Son, May 29, 1705?; dies May 30, 1705
    16: Martha, 1706 date not certain
    17: Charles, December 13, 1707
    18 and 19: Unknown sex and Kezia, March 1709?, the one twin dies that month.

The Family

A Guide for interpreting entries:

If a **full date** (month, date, year) appears at the beginning of the entry, that item belongs historically to that precise date.

Most **spelling** has been modernized and Americanized.

Where **text** has been deleted, it is represented by the customary three periods (...).

An asterisk (*) after a hymn or poem indicates that this is an excerpt only.

The book attempts to show the entire immediate family. However, despite the wealth of preserved written material, there is very little by some of the sisters. As for portraits, the popular evangelist John Wesley abounds: images of him proliferate like today's baseball cards or images on cereal boxes. But those who were not public figures and did not afford portraits in the age before the camera were not painted or engraved: there are no known likenesses of most of the sisters despite, for example, Hetty's renowned beauty. Never mind: the wonder is that we have as much as we do.

JANUARY

I rode to Epworth, which I still love beyond most places in the world. —John Wesley's *Journal. Above: The Old Rectory in Epworth, where the Wesleys lived for 39 years.*

1

January 1, 1777 We met, as usual, to renew our covenant with God. —John Wesley's *Journal*

2

January 2, 1770 Resolved by the grace of God, which I humbly beg in the name, and for the sake of the Lord Jesus; that from this day forward I will resign myself and all relations and secular concerns to the entire management of God's good providence; nor will I be anxious, or solicitous about events for the future, in things relating only to this life, Glory be to Thee, Oh Lord! —Susanna Wesley

3

Ye servants of God, your master proclaim
And publish abroad His wonderful name;
The name all-victorious of Jesus extol;
His kingdom is glorious, and rules over all.

Then let us adore, and give Him His right,
All glory and power, all wisdom and might,
All honor and blessing, with angels above,
And thanks never ceasing, and infinite love.*
—Charles Wesley, from *Hymns for Times of Trouble and Persecution* published in 1744, which bear direct reference to the brutal antagonism to which the Methodists were exposed and promise victory.

4

No music is to be heard upon earth comparable to the sound of many thousand voices when they are all harmoniously joined together singing praises to God and the Lamb.   —John Wesley's *Journal*

St. Andrew's Church, Epworth from an old print. Samuel Wesley was Rector here for 39 years.

5

Thou art never weary, O Lord, of doing us good. Let us never be weary of doing Thee service. Let us take pleasure in Thy service and abound in Thy work and in Thy love and praise evermore. Fill up all that is wanting, reform whatever is amiss in us, perfect the thing that concerneth us, and let the witness of Thy pardoning love ever abide in all our hearts.   —John Wesley

6

I cannot but stand amazed at the goodness of God. —John Wesley's *Journal*

7

She graced my humble roof, and blest my life,
Blest me by a far greater name than wife;
Yet still I bore an undisputed sway,
Nor was't her task, but pleasure, to obey;
Scarce thought, much less could act, what I denied,
In our low house there was no room for pride;
Nor need I e'er direct what still was right,
She studied my convenience and delight.
Nor did I for her care ungrateful prove,
But only used my power to show my love.
Whate'er she asked I gave,
    without reproach or grudge.
For still she reason asked,
    and I was judge;
All my commands, requests
    at her fair hands,
And her requests to me
    were all commands.
To others' households
    rarely she'd incline,
Her house her pleasure was,
    and she was mine.
Rarely abroad,
    or never but with me,
Or when by pity called, or charity.
    —Samuel Wesley's
    tribute to his wife

Susanna Wesley

January

8

Aim at the cheerfulness of faith. —John Wesley, Letter to Robert Carr Brackenbury

9

January 9, 1738 On Monday 9 and the following days, I reflected much on that vain desire, which had pursued me for so many years, of being in solitude, in order to be a Christian. I have now, thought I, solitude enough. But am I, therefore, the nearer being a Christian? Not if Jesus Christ be the model of Christianity. —John Wesley's *Journal*

10

1692 [December/January date uncertain] Emilia (Emily) born, 3rd child of Samuel and Susanna Wesley. Just before Emily married Robert Harper in 1735, her sister Hetty wrote a poem praising this eldest daughter:

> Virtue, Form, and Wit, in thee
> Move in perfect harmony....
> Thy virtues and thy graces all,
> How simple, free, and natural.
> Thy graceful form with pleasure I survey;
> It charms the eye — the heart, away ...
> To all thy outward majesty and grace,
> To all the blossoming features of thy face,
> To all the heavenly sweetness of thy mind,
> A noble, generous, equal soul is joined,
> By reason polished, and by arts refined.
> Thy even steady eye can see
> Dame Fortune smile, or frown, at thee.*

11

'Is thy heart right, as my heart is with thine?' I ask no farther question. 'If it be, give me thy hand.' For opinions, or terms, let us not 'destroy the work of God'. Does thou love and serve God? It is enough. I give thee the right hand of fellowship.   —John Wesley, *The Character of a Methodist* (1742)

January 12, 1766 I rode over to Kingswood; and, having told my whole mind to the masters and servants, spoke to the children in a far stronger manner than ever I did before. I will kill or cure: I will have one or the other, a Christian school, or none at all. —John Wesley's *Journal*

The school at Kingswood near Bristol, founded by the Methodist Societies.

January 13, 1710
Dear Sukey,
Since our misfortunes have separated us from each other, I can no other way comply with my inclination of doing you all the good I can, but by writing.

You know very well how I love you. I love your body; and do earnestly beseech Almighty God to bless it with health, and all things necessary for its comfort and support in this world. But my tenderest regard is for your immortal soul, and for its spiritual happiness; which regard I cannot better express than by endeavoring to instill into your mind those principles of knowledge and virtue that are absolutely necessary in order to your leading a good life here, which is the only thing that can infallibly secure your happiness hereafter. ...Anyone who makes a profession of religion, only because it is the custom of the country in which they live, or because their parents do so, or their worldly interest is thereby secured or advanced, will never be able to stand in the day of temptation; nor shall they ever enter into the kingdom of heaven.

Sukey, 'tis not learning these things by rote, nor the saying a few prayers morning and evening, that will bring you to heaven; you must understand what you say, and you must practise what you know. —Susanna Wesley to her daughter Susanna.
This remarkable letter goes on to give her lengthy interpretation of the Apostles' Creed.

14

January 14, 1772 I spent an agreeable hour with Dr. S, the oldest acquaintance I now have. He is the greatest genius in little things that ever fell under my notice. Almost everything about him is of his own invention, either in whole or in part. Even his fire-screen, his lamps of various sorts, his inkhorn, his very save-all. I really believe, were he seriously to set about it, he could invent the best mouse-trap that ever was in the world. —John Wesley's *Journal*

Engraving of Behemoth, from Samuel Wesley's 'Dissertations on the Book of Job'

15

To pursue after knowledge only for its own sake is a vain and unprofitable curiosity. To labor for it only to furnish matter of discourse, that you may be applauded by others, is still worse, and argues a vain-glorious, weak, and childish temper....Knowledge that goes no farther than speculation is like an excellent instrument in the hands of an unskilled person that knows not how to make use of it. Knowledge is indeed an admirable thing as it is the foundation or basis of wisdom....This wisdom you must earnestly pray for, and this is the use you must make of your knowledge. —Susanna Wesley

16

For how far is love, even with many wrong opinions, to be preferred before truth itself without love. We may die without the knowledge of many truths and yet be carried into Abraham's bosom. But if we do without love, what will knowledge avail? —John Wesley Preface to *Sermons on Several Occasions* (1746)

AN : ÆTAT: CERCITER LXX.

QUIS MIHI TRIBUAT

For years Samuel Wesley worked on his magnum opus, a thorough commentary on the times and social history of Job — military, medical, political, geographic, biological, etc. His volume was written in Latin, Greek and Hebrew. Engravings of animals and maps were specially commissioned, as well as this frontispiece where the author appears in classical pose amidst his subject matter.

18

Believe me, dear son, old age is the worst time we can choose to mend either our lives or our fortunes. If the foundations of solid piety are not laid betimes in sound principles and virtuous dispositions; and if we neglect, while strength and vigor lasts, to lay up something ere the infirmities of age overtake us, it is a hundred to one odds that we shall die both poor and wicked. —Susanna Wesley to John

---

19

Set a watch, O Lord, over my senses and appetites, my passions and understanding, that I may resolutely deny them every gratification which has no tendency to thy glory. Oh, train me up in this good way that, when I am old, I may not depart from it. —John Wesley

---

January

20

January 20, 1669 Susanna Annesley Wesley born, 25th child of The Rev. Samuel Annesley, Spitalfields, London

Help me to manage the common affairs of life in such a way as not to misemploy or neglect the improvement of my talents; to be industrious without covetousness; diligent without anxiety; as exact in each detail of action as if success were dependent on it, and yet so resigned as to leave all events to Thee and still attributing to Thee the praise of every good work.   —Susanna Wesley

21

To Treat Rheumatism: Steep six or seven cloves of garlic in half a pint of white wine. Drink it lying down. It sweats, and frequently cures at once.   —John Wesley, *Primitive Physic*

*John Wesley, age 40.
Engraving based on
Williams' portrait.*

My mother's reason for my cutting off my hair is because she fancies it prejudices my health. As to my looks, it would doubtless mend my complexion to have it off, by letting me get a little more color, and perhaps it might contribute to my making a more genteel appearance. But these, till ill health is added to them, I cannot persuade myself to be sufficient grounds for losing two or three pounds a year [to barbers and wigmakers].   —John Wesley to his brother Samuel, 1726

January 23 from Samuel Wesley, *An Account of Noises and Disturbances in my House at Epworth, Lincolnshire, in December and January, 1716* [the ghost they called "Old Jeffrey"]

From the first of December, my children and servants heard many strange noises, groans, knockings, &c, in every story, and most of the rooms of my house. But I hearing nothing of it myself, they would not tell me for some time, because, according to the vulgar opinion, if it boded any ill to me, I could not hear it. When it increased, and the family could not easily conceal it, they told me of it.

My daughters Susannah and Ann were below stairs in the dining room; and heard first at the doors, then over their heads, and the night after a knocking under their feet, though nobody was in the chambers or below them. The like they and my servants heard in both the kitchens, at the door against the partition, and over them. The maid servant heard groans as of a dying man. My daughter Emilia coming down stairs to draw up the clock and lock the doors at ten at night, as usual, heard under the staircase a sound among some bottles there, as if they had been all dashed to pieces; but when she looked, all was safe.

January 24, 1716, from Miss Susannah Wesley, a letter to her Brother Samuel, describing Old Jeffrey:

The first night I ever heard it, my sister Nancy and I were set in the dining room. We heard something rush on the outside of the doors that opened into the garden; then three loud knocks, immediately after other three, and in half a minute the same number over our heads. We inquired whether anybody had been in the garden, or in the room above us: but there was nobody. Soon after my sister Molly and I were up after all the family were abed, except my sister Nancy, about some business. We heard three bouncing thumps under our feet,

Signatures of the Wesley family, gathered in a composite by 19th century biographer Adam Clarke

which soon made us throw away our work, and tumble into bed. Afterwards, the tingling of the latch and warming pan, and so it took its leave that night.

I lay in the nursery, where it was very violent. I then heard frequent knocks over and under the room where I lay, and at the children's bed head, which was made of boards. It seemed to rap against it very hard and loud, so that the bed shook under them. I heard something walk by my bedside, like a man in a long night-gown....

It is now pretty quiet; only at our repeating the prayers for the king and prince, when it usually begins, especially when my father says, "Our most gracious Sovereign Lord," &c. This my father is angry at, and designs to say *three* instead of *two* for the royal family.

God's promises are sealed to us, but not dated: therefore patiently attend His pleasure. —Susanna Wesley to Charles

---

January 26, 1725   Immediately fall to work, read diligently the Hebrew text in the polyglot, and collate it exactly with the Vulgar Latin, which is in the second column, writing down all (even the least) variations or differences between them. To these I would have you add the Samaritan text in the last column but one, which is the very same with the Hebrew, except in some very few places, only differing in the Samaritan character (I think the true old Hebrew), the alphabet whereof you may learn in a day's time, either from the prolegomena in Walton's *Polyglot,* or from his grammar. In a twelvemonth's time, sticking close to it in the forenoons, you will get twice through the Pentateuch; for I have done it four times the last year, and am going over it the fifth, collating the Hebrew and two Greek, the Alexandrian and the Vatican, with what I can get of Symmachus and Theodotian, etc....

In the afternoon read what you will, and be sure to walk an hour, if fair, in the fields. —Samuel Wesley from Wroote to John at Oxford

---

January

27

Temptation exercises the man and fires the Christian. —Susanna Wesley

28

January 28, 1714   John Wesley enters Charterhouse school in London, age 10

29

How marvelous are the ways of God! How has He kept me even from a child! From ten to thirteen or fourteen, I had little but bread to eat, and not great plenty of that. I believe this was so far from hurting me, that it laid the foundation of lasting health. —John Wesley's *Journal*

30

January 30, 1740   Let me think and speak as a little child! Let my religion be plain, artless, simple! Meekness, temperance, patience, faith, and love, be these my highest gifts: and let the highest words wherein I teach them be those I learn from the Book of God! —John Wesley's *Journal*

31

January 31, 1696   Twins Annesley and Jedediah, 4th and 5th children, were born to Samuel and Susanna Wesley in December 1694 in South Ormsby. Annesley had died at one month. Today Jedediah dies.

January

FEBRUARY

John Wesley, engraving by George Vertue, 1745. Vertue also did engravings for Samuel Wesley. He is buried in Westminster Abbey. The scroll at the bottom shows the fire at Epworth Rectory and young John Wesley plucked as a brand from the burning.

1

February 1, 1738   John Wesley returns to England from Georgia.

2

I want to know one thing — the way to heaven: how to land safe on that happy shore. God himself has condescended to teach the way; for this very end He came from heaven. He hath written it down in a book. O give me that book! At any price, give me the book of God! I have it; here is knowledge enough for me. Let me be *homo unius libri* [a man of one book].   —John Wesley

3

February 3, 1744   The rioters lately summoned [the Methodists of Carlaston] by proclamation of the crier, to come to such a public house, and set to their hands that they would never hear the Methodist Preachers, or they should have their houses pulled down. About a hundred they compelled by blows. Notwithstanding which, both then and at other times, they have broken into their houses, robbing and destroying. And still if they hear any of them singing or reading the Scripture, they force open their doors by day and by night, and spoil and beat them with all impunity.   —Charles Wesley's *Journal*

4

Strengthen you one another. Talk together as often as you can. And pray earnestly with and for one another, that you may "endure to the end, and be saved."
—John Wesley, *A Plain Account of the People Called Methodists* (1749)

5

February 5, 1736   Charles Wesley lands in Georgia to serve as Secretary to Gov. Oglethorpe, and John Wesley to serve as a missionary to the Indians.

February 6, 1769   I spent an hour with a venerable woman near ninety years of age, who retains her health, her senses, her understanding, and even her memory, to a good degree. In the last century she belonged to my grandfather Annesley's congregation, at whose house her father and she used to dine every Thursday; and whom she remembers to have frequently seen in his study, at the top of the house, with his window open, and without any fire, winter or summer. He lived seventy-seven years, and would probably have lived longer had he not begun water-drinking at seventy.   —John Wesley's *Journal*

Dr. Samuel Annesley,
father of
Susanna Wesley

February 7, 1727   Martha Wesley, to her brother Jack:

Sister Emme is gone to Lincoln again, of which I'm very glad for her own sake; for she is weak and our misfortunes daily impair her health. Sister Kezzy, too, will have a fair chance of going. I believe if sister Molly stays long at home it will be because she can't get away. It is likely in a few years' time our family may be lessened, perhaps none left but your poor sister Martha, for whose welfare few are concerned.

February

8

February 8, 1750   A strong earthquake shakes London. "Such distress, perhaps, is not recorded to have happened before in this careless city," Charles writes, and he soon publishes *Hymns Occasion'd by the Earthquake.* One typical verse reads:

> Tremendous Lord of Earth and Skies,
> Most holy, high, and just,
> We fall before Thy glorious eyes,
> And hide us in the Dust:
> Thine Anger's long suspended Stroke
> With deepest Awe we feel,
> And tremble on, so lately shook
> Over the Mouth of Hell.*

9

February 9, 1709   A Fire at the Rectory in Epworth burns the Wesley home to the ground in fifteen minutes. John Wesley is, in his own account written years later, "a brand plucked from the burning." His father (pictured below) gives the most complete description:

On Wednesday last, at half an hour after eleven at night, in a quarter of an hour's time or less, my house at Epworth was burned down to the ground —I hope by accident; but God knows all. We had been brewing, but had done all; every spark of fire quenched before five o'clock that evening—at least six hours before the house was on fire. Perhaps the chimney above might take fire (though it had been swept not long since) and break through into the thatch. Yet it is strange I should neither see nor smell anything of it, having been in my study in that part of the house till above half an hour after ten. Then I locked the doors of that part of the house where my wheat and other corn lay, and went to bed.

The servants had not been in bed a quarter of an hour when the fire began. My wife being near her time, and very weak, I lay in the next chamber. A little after eleven I heard "Fire!" cried in the street, next to which I lay. If I had been in my own chamber, as usual, we had all been lost. I threw myself out of bed, got on my waistcoat and nightgown, and looked out of window; saw the reflection of the flame, but I knew not where it was; ran to my wife's chamber with one stocking on and my breeches in my hand; would have broken open the door, which was bolted within, but could not. My two eldest children were with her [Emilia and Susanna]. They rose and ran towards the staircase, to raise the rest of the house. There I saw it was my own house, all in a light blaze, and nothing but a door between the flame and the staircase.

I ran back to my wife, who by this time had got out of bed, naked, and opened the door. I bade her fly for her life. We had a little silver and some gold—about £20. She would have stayed for it, but I pushed her out; got her and my two eldest children downstairs (where two of the servants were now got), and asked for the keys. They knew nothing of them. I ran upstairs and found them, came down, and opened the street door. The thatch was fallen in all on fire. The north-east wind drove all the sheets of flame in my face, as if reverberated in a lamp. I got twice to the steps and was drove down again. I ran to the garden door and opened it. The fire there was more moderate. I bade them all follow, but found only two with me, and the maid with another [Charles] in her arms that cannot go; but all naked. I ran with them to an outhouse in the garden, out of the reach of the flames; put the least in the other's lap; and not finding my wife follow me, ran back into the house to seek her, but could not find her. The servants and two of the children were got out at the window. In the kitchen I found my eldest

daughter, naked, and asked her for her mother. She could not tell me where she was. I took her up and carried her to the rest in the garden; came in the second time and ran upstairs, the flame breaking through the wall at the staircase; thought all my children were safe, and hoped my wife was some way got out. I then remembered my books, and felt in my pocket for the key of the chamber which led to my study. I could not find the key, though I searched a second time. Had I opened that door, I must have perished.

I ran down and went to my children in the garden, to help them over the wall. When I was without, I heard one of my poor lambs, left still above-stairs, about six years old [Jacky], cry out, dismally, "Help me!" I ran in again, to go upstairs, but the staircase was now all afire. I tried to force up through it a second time, holding my breeches over my head, but the stream of fire beat me down. I thought I had done my duty; went out of the house to that part of my family I had saved, in the garden, with the killing cry of my child in my ears. I made them all kneel down, and we prayed to God to receive his soul.

I tried to break down the pales, and get my children over into the street, but could not; then went under the flame and got them over the wall. Now I put on my breeches and leaped after them. One of my maidservants that had brought out the least child, got out much at the same time. She was saluted with a hearty curse by one of the neighbors, and told that we had fired the house ourselves, the second time, on purpose! I ran about inquiring for my wife and other children; met the chief man and chief constable of the town going from my house, not towards it to help me. I took him by the hand and said, "God's will be done!" His answer was, "Will you never have done your tricks? You fired your house once before; did you not get enough by it then, that you have done it again?" This was cold comfort. I said, "God forgive you! I find you are chief man still." But I had a little better soon after, hearing that my wife was saved; and then I fell on mother earth and blessed God.

I went to her. She was alive, and could just speak. She thought I had perished, and so did all the rest, not having seen me nor any share of eight children for a quarter of an hour; and by this time all the chambers and everything was consumed to ashes, for the fire was stronger than a furnace, the violent wind beating it down on the house. She told me afterwards how she escaped. When I went first to open the back door, she endeavored to force through the fire at the fore door, but was struck back twice to the ground. She thought to have died there, but prayed to Christ to help her. She found new strength, got up alone and waded through two or three yards of flame, the fire on the ground being up to her knees. She had nothing on but her shoes and a wrapping gown, and one coat on her arm. This she wrapped about her breast, and got through safe into the yard, but no soul yet to help her.

She never looked up or spake till I came; only when they brought her last child to her, bade them lay it on the bed. This was the lad whom I heard cry in the house, but God saved him almost by a miracle. He only was forgot by the servants, in the hurry. He ran to the window towards the yard, stood upon a chair and cried for help. There were now a few people gathered, one of whom, who loves me, helped up another to the window. The child seeing a man come into the window, was frightened, and ran away to get to his mother's chamber. He could not open the door, so ran back again. The man was fallen down from the window, and all the bed and hangings in the room where he was were blazing. They helped up the man a second time, and poor Jacky leaped into his arms and was saved. I could not believe it till I had kissed him two or three times. My wife then said unto me, "Are your books safe?" I told her it was not much, now she and all the rest were preserved....

Mr. Smith of Gainsborough, and others, have sent for some of my children....I want nothing, having above half my barley saved in my barns unthreshed. I had finished my alterations in the *Life of Christ* a little while since, and transcribed three copies of it. But all is lost. God be praised!

I hope my wife will recover, and not miscarry, but God will give me my nineteenth child. She has burnt her legs, but they mend. When I came to her, her lips were black. I did not know her. Some of the children are a little burnt, but not hurt or disfigured. I only got a small blister on my hand. The neighbors send us clothes, for it is cold without them.

February 10, 1690   Samuel Wesley, Jr., born, first child of Samuel and Susanna Wesley, in London.

He did not speak until he was five. One day when his anxious parents could not find him, suddenly his voice piped from under a table, "Here I am!" and thereafter he spoke without difficulty. Samuel was born with a mark resembling a mulberry on his neck. John wrote that "every spring it was small and white, it then grew larger, as the fruit itself grew, first green, then red, then a deep purple, as large and as deep a color as a mulberry on the tree."

Receive me, O God, as a brand snatched out of the fire.
—John Wesley

Mr. Wesley rebuilt his house in less than one year; but nearly thirteen years are elapsed since it was burned, yet it is not half furnished, nor his wife and children half clothed to this day. —Susanna Wesley, to her brother Samuel in India

February

13

Do all the good you can,
By all the means you can,
In all the ways you can,
In all the places you can,
At all the times you can,
To all the people you can,
As long as ever you can.
—John Wesley's *Rule*

14

February 14, 1727 John Wesley graduated M.A., from Oxford

15

Then I came home again in an evil hour for me. I was well clothed, and, while I wanted nothing, was easy enough....Thus far we went on tolerably well; but this winter, when my own necessaries began to decay, and my money was most of it spent (I having maintained myself since I came home, but now could do it no longer), I found what a condition I was in: every trifling want was either not suppplied, or I had more trouble to procure it than it was worth. I know not when we have had so good a year, both at Wroote and at Epworth, as this year; but, instead of saving anything to clothe my sisters or myself, we are just where we were. A noble crop has almost all gone, beside Epworth living, to pay some part of those infinite debts my father has run into, which are so many, as I have lately found out, that were he to save fifty pounds a year he would not be clear in the world this seven years....Yet in this distress we enjoy many comforts. We have plenty of good meat and drink, fuel, etc., have no duns, nor any of that tormenting care for to provide bread which we had at Epworth. In short, could I lay aside all thought of the future, and could be content without three things, money, liberty, and clothes, I might live very comfortably.   —Emilia to John, 1725

February

from *Lines Written When in Deep Anguish of Spirit*
Enable me to bear my lot,
Oh Thou who only cans't redress!
Eternal God! forsake me not
In this extreme of my distress.
Regard thy humble suppliant's suit;
Nor let me long in anguish pine,
Dismayed, abandoned, destitute
Of all support, but only Thine!
Nor health, nor life, I ask of Thee;
Nor languid nature to restore:
Say but "a speedy period be
To these thy griefs," —I ask no more!*
    —Mehetabel "Hetty" Wesley Wright

Always take advice or reproof as a favor; it is the surest mark of love.   —John Wesley

February 18, 1726   Hetty's first child, a girl, is baptized.

February 19, 1751   John Wesley marries Mrs. Mary Vazeille, a merchant's widow who has four children. She had nursed him in her home in Threadneedle Street when he badly sprained an ankle. It is not a good match, she is jealous of his work, and after several years they cease to live together.

February

20

Do good unto all men. Snatch all the opportunities you can of speaking a word to any of your neighbors. Comfort the afflicted, support the weak, exhort the believers to go on to perfection. Never be weary of well doing; in due time you shall reap if you faint not. —John Wesley, Letter to Jane Barton

21

February 21, 1782   At our yearly meeting for that purpose, we examined our yearly accounts, and found the money received (just answering the expense) was upwards of three thousand pounds a year. But that is nothing to me: what I receive of it is neither more nor less than thirty pounds. —John Wesley's *Journal*

The Market Cross in Epworth. John Wesley preached on its steps a number of times.

22

February 22, 1791   John Wesley preaches his last sermon.

23

I scarce ever yet repented of saying too little, but frequently of saying too much. —John Wesley, Letter to Samuel Furley

February 24, 1791   John Wesley makes the last entry in his diary and writes his last letter, to William Wilberforce:

Dear Sir,

Unless the divine power has raised you up to be as *Athanasius contra mundum* [Athanasius against the world], I see not how you can go through your glorious enterprise in opposing that execrable villany, which is the scandal of religion, of England, and of human nature. Unless God has raised you up for this very thing, you will be worn out by the opposition of men and devils. But if God be for you, who can be against you? Are all of them together stronger than God? O be not weary of well doing! Go on, in the name of God and in the power of his might, till even American slavery (the vilest that ever saw the sun) shall vanish away before it.

Reading this morning a tract wrote by a poor African, I was particularly struck by that circumstance, that a man who has a black skin, being wronged or outraged by a white man, can have no redress; it being a *law* in all our Colonies that the *oath* of a black against a white goes for nothing. What villany is this!

That He who has guided you from youth up may continue to strengthen you in this and all things is the prayer of, dear sir,
Your affectionate servant,
John Wesley

25

February 25th, 1725 Dear Jackey, I was much pleased with your letter to your father about taking Orders, and like the proposal well; but it is an unhappiness almost peculiar to our family that your father and I seldom think alike. I approve the disposition of your mind and think the sooner you are a deacon the better, because it may be an inducement to greater application in the study of practical divinity, which I humbly conceive is the best study for candidates for orders. Mr. Wesley differs from me, and would engage you (I believe) in critical learning; which, though accidentally of use, is in no wise preferable to the other. —Susanna Wesley

26

Let all things be done in love. —Charles Wesley

27

Beck must recover her music; most positively, or not look me in the face. It lies upon you to drag her to the harpsichord, and tie her down in her chair. —Charles Wesley to his wife, referring to her sister Rebecca

28

February 28, 1784 John Wesley executes the "Deed of Declaration," the charter of Wesleyan Methodism. Trustees of local chapels wanted to choose their own preachers. Wesley drew up this deed in the Court of High Chancery to provide for a conference of 100 preachers (the controversial "Legal Hundred") who would exercise the powers Wesley had previously reserved for himself.

Opposite page: Engraving by William Ridley based on miniature by Arnold. This is apparently the portrait referred to by Wesley in his Journal for February 22, 1790: "I could scarcely believe myself. The picture of one in his eighty-seventh year!"

MARCH

March 1 'The Holy Triumph of John Wesley in His Dying' painted by Marshall Claxton, R.A., who showed the picture at the Royal Academy of 1842. Although Wesley's small bedroom could not have accommodated all these people at once, they are among those who visited him in his last days. Sarah Wesley is at far left, her mother kneeling at the foot of the bed.

1

March 2, 1792   John Wesley dies in his home in City Road, London after a final illness of five days. Even in his weakness he sings a final hymn, "I'll Praise My Maker While I've Breath." He is buried in a plot behind City Road chapel by night, for fear of unmanageably large crowds. Several other early Methodist preachers are interred in the same vault and share the same marker. Modern buildings constructed behind the Chapel have been designed sensitive to the site; rather than overwhelm it, their glass walls reflect and seem to enlarge the grounds.

2

3

March 3, 1709 (probable date) Kezziah born, 19th child of Samuel and Susanna, in Epworth.

4

Nothing but grace can keep our children, after our departure, from running into a thousand sects, a thousand errors....Especially family and private prayer, and sacrament, will keep them steady. Let us labor, while we continue here, to ground and build them up in the Scriptures, and all the ordinances. —Charles Wesley's *Journal*

5

March 5, 1738 I asked [Peter] Bohler whether he thought I should leave [off preaching] or not. He answered, "By no means." I asked, "But what can I preach?" He said, "Preach faith till you have it; and then, because you have it, you will preach faith." —John Wesley's *Journal*

6

Tradition says that Charles Wesley may have written this hymn upon seeing the colliery fires near Newcastle on one of his many trips to the north:

> **See how great a flame aspires**
> Kindled by a spark of grace!
> Jesu's love the nations fires,
> Sets the kingdoms on a blaze.
> To bring fire on earth he came
> Kindled in some hearts it is:
> O that all might catch the flame,
> All partake the glorious bliss!
>
> Saw ye not the cloud arise,
> Little as a human hand?
> Now it spreads along the skies,
> Hangs o'er all the thirsty land;
> Lo! the promise of a shower
> Drops already from above;
> But the Lord will shortly pour
> All the spirit of His love.*
> —Charles Wesley

7

Sing lustily and with a good courage. Beware of singing as if you were half dead, or half asleep; but lift up your voice with strength.   —John Wesley, *Directions for Singing* as printed in the Hymn Book in 1761

8

For Hoarseness: Rub the soles of the feet before the fire, with garlic and lard well beaten together, over night. The hoarseness will be gone next day. Or, instead of supper, eat an apple and drink half a pint of water. Or, swallow slowly the juice of radishes; or take a spoonful of sage juice morning and evening.   —John Wesley, *Primitive Physic*

9

March 9, 1746 I got abroad again after my painful confinement with the toothache, and officiated at the chapel. —Charles Wesley's *Journal*

10

March 10, 1741 Yesterday morning sister Kezzy died in the Lord Jesus. He finished His work, and cut it short for mercy. Full of thankfulness, resignation, and love, without pain or trouble, she commended her spirit into the hands of Jesus, and fell asleep. —Charles Wesley's *Journal*

11

Faith is that divine evidence whereby the spiritual man discerneth God and the things of God. It is with regard to the spiritual world what sense is with regard to the natural. It is the spiritual sensation of every soul that is born of God. —John Wesley, *An Earnest Appeal to Men of Reason and Religion* (1743)

12

March 12, 1733 Charles graduated M.A., Oxford

March

13

The parish of Wroote was added to Samuel Wesley's curacy in 1724, at a salary of £50. For several years the family lived in its smaller rectory, Rev. Wesley commuting through marshes by horse, foot, or boat.

The Rectory at Wroote

14

Samuel, Jr., penned these lines about Wroote in the popular style of romantic exaggeration.

> The House is good, and strong, and clean,
> Tho' there no battlements are seen,
> But humble roof of thatch, I ween,
>   Low rooms from rain to cover.
> Where safe from poverty, (sore ill!)
> All may live happy if they will,
> As any that St. James's fill,
>   Th'Escurial, or the Louvre.
>
> What happiness! then to be driven
> Where powers of *saving* may be given!
> To hope for unmolested heaven
>   While here on earth — too soon is:
> But this is certain, if you're wise,
> Wroote is the seat of Paradise,
> As much as any place that lies
>   On earth beside the moon is.*

March 15, 1779   I began my tour through England and Scotland; the lovely weather continuing, such as the oldest man alive had not seen before, for January, February, and half of March. —John Wesley's *Journal*

15

Help me to overcome habitual levity in my thoughts. —Susanna Wesley *Meditations*

16

March 17, 1726   John Wesley elected Fellow of Lincoln College, Oxford. It provides a stipend that continues until he marries. His father writes proudly, "Wherever I am, my Jack is Fellow of Lincoln."

17

Engraving from Samuel Wesley's 'Dissertations on the Book of Job.' In this detail, the figure praying (toward the top) is Abraham. The city on the hill at bottom is Masada.

March 18, 1740   We spent an hour in songs of triumph. —Charles Wesley's *Journal*

18

March 19, 1742   I rode once more to Pensford, at the earnest request of several serious people. The place where they desired me to preach was a little green spot, near the town. But I had no sooner begun, than a great company of rabble, hired (as we afterward found) for

that purpose, came furiously upon us, bringing a bull, which they had been baiting, and now strove to drive in among the people.

But the beast was wiser than his drivers; and continually ran either on one side of us, or the other, while we quietly sang praise to God and prayed for about an hour. The poor wretches, finding themselves disappointed, at length seized upon the bull, now weak and tired, after having been so long torn and beaten both by dogs and men; and, by main strength, partly dragged and partly thrust him in among the people.

When they had forced their way to the little table on which I stood, they strove several times to throw it down, by thrusting the helpless beast against it; who, of himself, stirred no more than a log of wood. I once or twice put aside his head with my hand, that the blood might not drop upon my clothes; intending to go on as soon as the hurry should be a little over.

But the table falling down, some of our friends caught me in their arms and carried me right away on their shoulders; while the rabble wreaked their vengeance on the table, which they tore bit from bit. We went a little way off, where I finished my discourse without any noise or interruption.   —John Wesley's *Journal*

I have long ardently wished for death, because, you know, we Methodists always die in a transport of joy.
—Hetty Wesley Wright

March 21, 1750   Mehetabel Wesley Wright (Hetty) dies in London, age 53.

At four I called on my brother Wright [Hetty's husband], a few minutes after her spirit was set at liberty. I had sweet fellowship with her in explaining at the chapel those solemn words, 'Thy sun shall no more go down, neither shall thy moon withdraw itself; for the Lord shall be thy everlasting light, and the days of thy mourning shall be ended.'   —Charles Wesley's *Journal*

AN EPITAPH ON HERSELF
[By Mrs. Wright: Mehetabel Wesley]

Destin'd while living to sustain
An equal share of grief and pain;
All various ills of human race
Within this breast had once a place.
Without complaint she learn'd to bear
A living death, a long despair;
Till hard oppress'd by adverse fate,
O'ercharg'd, she sunk beneath its weight;
And to this peaceful tomb retired,
So much esteem'd, so long desired.
The painful mortal conflict's o'er:
A broken heart can bleed no more!

23

Your father is in a very bad state of health; he sleeps little and eats less. He seems not to have any apprehension of his approaching exit, but I fear he has but a short time to live. It is with much pain and difficulty that he performs Divine Service on the Lord's Day, which sometimes he is obliged to contract very much. Everybody observes his decay but himself, and people really seem much concerned for him and his family. —Susanna Wesley to John

24

How uneasy is my mind, O God, when either company, business, or anything else diverts it from its usual course. I praise Thee for suffering me to meet with no more interruption and am thankful for daily opportunities and common mercies that are often unregarded. Forgive me and enable me to see that the more common the mercy the more valuable it is. —Susanna Wesley

Susanna Wesley, from a posthumous
portrait by J.W.L. Forster

Lor! th' Eternal Word I sing,
Whose great Spirit my Breast inspire.
Whilst I touch the sounding string
Tune, some Angel! Tune my lyre!
Rise, my Eagle-Soul! arise!
Mount and mean thy native Skies,
And view th' eternal Sun with thy ambitious Eyes!
(If once direct his Glories on me shin'd,
How gladly wou'd I be for ever Blind?)
    —from Samuel Wesley's *Life of Christ*

Entire sanctification, or Christian perfection, is neither more nor less than pure love ... love expelling sin and governing both the heart and life of a child of God. The Refiner's fire purges out all that is contrary to love, and that many times by a pleasing smart.   —John Wesley, Letter to Walter Churchey

I think myself bound in duty to add my testimony to my brother's. His twelve reasons against our ever separating from the Church of England are mine also. I subscribe to them with all my heart....My affection for the Church is as strong as ever: and I clearly see my calling, which is to live and die in her communion. This, therefore, I am determined to do, the Lord being my helper. —Charles Wesley, in response to John's *Reasons against a Separation from the Church of England*

March

Behind City Road Chapel, London. Spanning centuries, the graveyard, Wesley's monument, and the chapel itself are reflected in new glass buildings.

March 28, 1739   I look upon all the world as my parish;
thus far I mean, that in whatever part of it I am, I judge
it meet, right, and my bounden duty to declare unto all
that are willing to hear, the glad tidings of salvation.
This is the work which I know God has called me to do.
And sure I am that His blessing attends it.   —John
Wesley, Letter to John Clayton

*Pictured above, the statue of John Wesley in front of City
Road Chapel*

March

29

March 29, 1788   Charles Wesley dies, age 80. He is buried April 5 in Marylebone parish churchyard. A few days before his death, he dictated his final poem to his wife:

> In age and feebleness extreme,
> Who shall a sinful worm redeem?
> Jesus, my only hope Thou art,
> Strength of my failing flesh and heart.
> O could I catch a smile from Thee,
> And drop into eternity!

Charles had earlier written to John, "We have taken each other for better for worse, till death do us —part? No; but unite eternally."

30

March 30, 1734   Heaven is a State as well as a Place; a state of Holiness, begun in this life, though not perfected till we enter upon Life eternal.... All Sins are so many spiritual diseases, which must be cured by the power of Christ, before we can be capable of being happy....
When I begin to write to you, I think I don't know how to make an end.... Pray give my Love and Blessing to Charles. I hope he is well, though I have never heard from him since he left Epworth.   —Susanna Wesley to John

---

31

March 31, 1739   In the evening I reached Bristol, and met Mr. Whitefield there. I could scarce reconcile myself at first to this strange way of preaching in the fields, of which he set me an example on Sunday; having been all my life (till very lately) so tenacious of every point relating to decency and   order, that I should have thought the saving of souls almost a sin, if it had not been done in a church.   —John Wesley's *Journal*

Westminster School, London.

April 1, 1739 In the evening (Mr. Whitefield being gone) I begun expounding our Lord's Sermon on the Mount (one pretty remarkable precedent of field-preaching, though I suppose there were churches at that time also). —John Wesley's *Journal*

1

Methinks 'tis a pity we should lose any time, for what a vapor is life! —John Wesley, Letter to John Fletcher

2

Palm Sunday 1710 As the love and goodness of God is altogether incomprehensible, so is it wonderful to observe the little effect it hath upon the children of men. How small impression the sufferings and death of Christ make upon the minds of the generality of the world. —Susanna Wesley

3

April 4, 1736   About four in the afternoon I set out for Frederica in a pettiawga, a sort of flat-bottomed barge. The next evening we anchored near Skidoway Island, where the water, at flood, was twelve or fourteen feet deep. I wrapped myself up from head to foot in a large cloak, to keep off the sandflies, and lay down on the quarterdeck. Between one and two I waked under water, being so fast asleep that I did not find where I was till my mouth was full of it. Having left my cloak, I know not how, upon deck, I swam round to the other side of the pettiawga, where a boat was tied, and climbed up by the rope without any hurt, more than wetting my clothes.
—John Wesley's *Journal* in Georgia

April 5, 1788   Charles Wesley buried in Marylebone churchyard. On the road, John does not hear of the death in time to attend the funeral. He writes to an assistant, "'Tis pity but the remains of my brother had been deposited with me. Certainly the ground [at City Road] is holy as any in England, and it contains a large quantity of 'bonny dust'." But Charles had specified, "I have lived and I die in the communion of the Church of England, and I will be buried in the yard of my parish church."

Monument behind Marylebone church to Charles Wesley

Dick [Ellison] is (if possible) 'tenfold more the child of Hell' than he used to be. He took it into his head 'tother night almost to beat out his wife's brains for taking his man off of him that was going to murder him. —Martha Wesley to John, 1730, referring to her sister Sukey's husband

April 7, 1746 I preached at Kingswood and laid the first stone of the new house there. —John Wesley's *Journal*

April 8, 1749 Charles marries Sarah (Sally) Gwynne, nineteen years his junior, at Llanlleonfel Church. It is a happy marriage. The couple lives in Bristol, then London. They have eight children, three of whom survive: Charles, Samuel, and Sarah.

"Sweet day! so cool, so calm, so bright,
The bridal of the earth and sky."
Not a cloud was to be seen from morning till night. I rose at four; spent three hours and an half in prayer, or singing with my brother, with Sally, with Beck [Sally's sister Rebecca]. At eight I led my Sally to church. Her father, sisters, Lady Rudd, Grace Bowen, Betty Williams, and, I think, Billy Tucker, and Mrs. James, were all the persons present." —Charles Wesley's *Journal*

Charles and Sarah Wesley's home in Bristol

April

Sarah (Sally) Gwynne, married to Charles Wesley 1749

9

April 9, 1742   We had the first watchnight in London. We commonly choose for this solemn service the Friday night nearest the full moon, either before or after, that those of the congregation who live at a distance may have light to their several homes. The service begins at half an hour past eight, and continues till a little after midnight. We have often found a peculiar blessing at these seasons. There is generally a deep awe upon the congregation, perhaps in some measure owing to the silence of the night, particularly in singing the hymn with which we commonly conclude—

> Hearken to the solemn voice,
> The Awful midnight cry!
> Waiting souls, rejoice, rejoice,
> And feel the Bridegroom nigh.
> —John Wesley's *Journal*

Christ the Lord is risen today. Alleluia!
Sons of men and angels say Alleluia!
Raise your joys and triumphs high! Alleluia!
Sing, ye heavens, and earth reply Alleluia!

Lives again our glorious King. Alleluia!
Where, O death, is now thy sting? Alleluia!
Once He died our souls to save Alleluia!
Where's thy victory, boasting grave? Alleluia!

Love's redeeming work is done Alleluia!
Fought the fight, the battle won. Alleluia!
Death in vain forbids Him rise. Alleluia!
Christ hath opened Paradise! Alleluia!

Soar we now where Christ has led, Alleluia!
Following our exalted head. Alleluia!
Made like Him, like Him we rise! Alleluia!
Ours the cross, the grave, the skies! Alleluia!*
    —Charles Wesley

April 11, 1760   Yesterday evening I buried my brother
Ellison [Susanna's husband]. Sister Macdonald, who he
was always very fond of, prayed by him in his last
moments. He told her he was not afraid to die, and
believed God, for Christ's sake, had forgiven him. I felt
a most solemn awe while I committed his body to the
earth.   —Charles Wesley to his wife

By Methodists I mean a people who profess to pursue (in
whatsoever measure they have attained) holiness of
heart and life, inward and outward conformity in all
things to the revealed will of God; who place religion in
an uniform resemblance of the great object of it; in a
steady imitation of Him they worship in all his imitable
perfections; more particularly in justice, mercy, and
truth, or universal love filling the heart, and governing
the life.   —John Wesley, *Advice to the People Called
Methodists* (1745)

April

13

Dr. Samuel Annesley, father of Susanna Annesley Wesley

It is serious Christianity that I press, as the only way to better every condition: it is Christianity, downright Christianity, that alone can do it: it is not morality without faith; that is but refined Heathenism: it is not faith without morality: that is but downright hypocrisy: it must be a divine faith, wrought by the Holy Ghost, where God and man concur in the operation; such a faith as works by love, both to God and man; a holy faith, full of good works.   —Dr. Samuel Annesley

14

There's no Time for preparing for Heaven like the Time of Youth. Though Death were never so near, I can look back with Joy on some of the early years that I sweetly spent in my Father's House, and how I comfortably lived there. O what a mercy it is to be Dedicated to God betimes!   —Elizabeth Annesley, Susanna Wesley's sister

15

April 1736 I heartily wish you may...have provided for my mother's subsistence, if I should die. If you have not taken care of her, if surviving me, 'tis a guilty, a very guilty omission, which I would not have willingly been stained with, no, not to convert a continent. —Samuel Wesley, Jr., to John in America regarding their mother's arrest for debt after their father's death

16

How, then, is it possible that Methodism, that is, the religion of the heart, though it flourishes now as a green bay tree, should continue in this state? For the Methodists in every place grow diligent and frugal; consequently, they increase in goods. Hence they proportionably increase in pride, in anger, in the desire of the flesh, the desire of the eyes, and the pride of life. So although the form of religion remains, the spirit is swiftly vanishing away. —John Wesley, *Thoughts upon Methodism* (1786)

17

April 17, 1776 Faith is given according to our present need. You have now such faith as is necessary for your living unto God. As yet you are not called to die. When you are, you shall have faith for this also. Today improve the faith which you now have, and trust God with tomorrow. —John Wesley, Letter to Mary Bishop

18

Gain all you can, without hurting either yourself or your neighbor, in soul or body, by applying hereto with unintermitted diligence, and with all the understanding which God has given you. *Save all you can,* by cutting off every expense which serves only to indulge foolish desire, to gratify either the desire of the flesh, the desire of the eye, or the pride of life. Waste nothing, living or dying, on sin or folly, whether for yourself or your children. And then, *Give all you can,* or in other words give all you have, to God. —John Wesley Sermon 50, *The Use of Money* (1760)

April

19

You do not consider, money never stays with me; it would burn me if it did. I throw it out of my hands as soon as possible, lest it should find a way into my heart.
—John Wesley, Letter to his sister Martha

20

I rode to Craidley. In the following days I went on slowly, through Stafford-shire and Cheshire, to Manchester. In this journey, as well as in many others, I observed a mistake that almost universally prevails; and I desire all travellers to take good notice of it, which may save them both from trouble and danger. Near thirty years ago, I was thinking, "How is it that no horse ever stumbles while I am reading?" (History, poetry, and philosophy I commonly read on horseback, having other employment at other times.) No account can possibly be given but this: because then I throw the reins on his neck. I then set myself to observe; and I aver that in riding above an hundred thousand miles, I scarce ever remember any horse (except two, that would fall head over heels any way) to fall, or make a considerable stumble, while I rode with a slack rein. To fancy, therefore, that a tight rein prevents stumbling is a capital blunder. I have repeated the trial more frequently than most men in the kingdom can do. A slack rein will prevent stumbling if anything will. But in some horses nothing can. —John Wesley's *Journal*

April 21, 1787   With what is past or what is to come we have little to do. *Now* is the day of salvation.   —John Wesley, Letter to John King

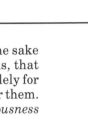

21

All believers are forgiven and accepted, not for the sake of anything in them, or of anything that ever was, that is, or ever can be done by them, but wholly and solely for the sake of what Christ hath done and suffered for them. —John Wesley, Sermon 20, *The Lord Our Righteousness* (1765)

22

April 23, 1738   John Wesley prays "Lord, help Thou my unbelief!"   —John Wesley's *Journal*

23

April 24, 1769   Mend your clothes, or I shall never expect you to mend your lives. Let none ever see a ragged Methodist.   —John Wesley, Letter to Richard Steel

24

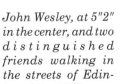

John Wesley, at 5"2" in the center, and two distinguished friends walking in the streets of Edinburgh in 1790

April

April 25, 1735 Samuel Wesley dies at Epworth. He is buried in the graveyard of St. Andrew's, where he had served 39 years. Written by Susanna, his epitaph reads:

Here lyeth all that was Mortal of
Samuel Wesley, A.M.
He was rector of Epworth 39 years,
and departed this Life 25 of April 1735. Aged 72.
As he liv'd so he died, in the true Catholic Faith
of the holy Trinity in Unity,
And that Jesus Christ is God incarnate:
and the only Saviour of Mankind. Acts iv 12.
Blessed are the dead which die in the Lord, yea, saith
the Spirit, that they may rest from their labours and
Their works do follow them. Rev xiv 13.

Samuel Wesley's tombstone in the graveyard of St. Andrew's, as it was. It now stands apart from other graves.

The inward witness, son, the inward witness, this is the proof, the strongest proof of Christianity. —Samuel Wesley on his deathbed, to John

What is moral liberty? Rectitude of mind. When the mind is as it should be, free from all error and sins. Habits of sin are the chains or fetters of the soul, which deprive it of its native liberty, and seduce it to a true state of captivity, which while it is under it hath no more power to act as it ought to do than a body bound with chains or iron can follow its usual labor. —Susanna Wesley

28

[from **Earth, rejoice, our Lord is King**]
Christ the Saviour is come down,
Points us to the victor's crown,
Bids us take our seats above,
More than conquerors in His love.*
   —Charles Wesley

29

Your next step grieves me and would astonish me if I had not left wondering for some time. You and Charles are trying how a vegetable diet will agree with you. For what? You cannot imagine you have the same call to it that Daniel had to refuse the King's provision. It cannot be religion, for abstaining from meats is a doctrine of Devils and well may it be called so peculiarly in the present case, since 'tis arrogant and sullen, dashing back again to God's own grant after the flood. It cannot be policy, in my humble opinion, unless you had not a sufficient stock on board. Otherwise 'tis quite contrary to common sense to weaken your strength and spirits (as vegetable food comparatively must do) at the very time when your work is increasing. —Samuel Wesley, Jr., to John Wesley in Georgia

30

Dear Brother,
You may remember when you was here your asking me whether I have advised any of my acquaintance to fasting. I have not yet, for two reasons. First because people are so averse to the giving themselves pain, that there's scarce a possibility of my prevailing with any to act contrary to what they have been used to. The second is I meet with such discouragement myself that I can but just stand my ground; if I be ill whither it proceeds from cold or any other cause, 'tis always imputed my abstemious way of living. So as fasting is not an essential part of religion, but only an instrumental duty, if people can attain the end without using the means, I can't see any necessity for performing this duty....
—Yours till death,
Kezia Wesley

April

Reverend John Wesley by George Romney. In his Journal for January 5, 1789, Wesley writes "At the earnest desire of Mrs. T——, I once more sat for my picture. Mr. Romney is a painter indeed. He struck off an exact likeness at once; and did more in one hour than Sir Joshua did in ten." Romney's portrait is the model for numerous other paintings, engravings, and drawings.

April

MAY

Charles Wesley, by John Russell, R.A.

May 1, 1780   John Wesley publishes *A Collection of
Hymns for the Use of the People Called Methodists*

1

2

In May 1739, Charles Wesley writes this hymn to commemorate the first anniversary of his own inner conversion and rebirth. The familiar opening stanza was originally the 7th of 18 verses.

O for a thousand tongues to sing
My great Redeemer's praise,
The glories of my God and King,
The triumphs of His grace!

My gracious Master and my God,
Assist me to proclaim,
To spread through all the earth abroad
The honors of Thy name.

Jesus! the name that charms our fears,
That bids our sorrows cease;
'Tis music in the sinner's ears,
'Tis life, and health, and peace.

He speaks, and, listening to His voice,
New life the dead receive,
The mournful, broken hearts rejoice,
The humble poor believe.

He breaks the power of cancelled sin,
He sets the prisoner free;
His blood can make the foulest clean,
His blood availed for me.*

[The original first verse is:]
Glory to God, and praise and love
Be ever, ever given
By saints below and saints above,
The Church in earth and heaven.

3

You must remember you cannot be warm alone; you must needs find one if not more with whom you can converse freely on the things of God.   —John Wesley, Letter to Harriet Lewis

Religion has nothing sour, austere, unsociable, unfriendly in it, but on the contrary implies the most winning sweetness, the most amiable softness and gentleness. —John Wesley, Letter to Mary Chapman

T. A. Dean's engraving based on John Jackson's painting of John Wesley

May 5, 1784 [In Aberdeen] I found the morning preaching had been long discontinued; yet the bands and the select society were kept up. But many were faint and weak for want of morning preaching and prayer-meetings, of which I found scarce any traces in Scotland. In the evening I talked largely with the preachers, and showed them the hurt it did both to them and the people for any one preacher to stay six or eight weeks together in one place. Neither can he find matter for preaching every morning and evening, nor will the people come to hear him. Hence he grows cold by lying in bed, and so do the people. Whereas if he never stays more than a fortnight together in one place, he may find matter enough, and the people will gladly hear him. They immediately drew up such a plan for this Circuit, which they determined to pursue. —John Wesley's *Journal*

May

6

If ever any child performed an act of obedience, or did anything with an intention to please, though the performance was not well, yet the obedience and intention should be kindly accepted, and the child with sweetness directed how to do better for the future. —Susanna Wesley

7

May 7, 1741   I reminded the United Society that many of our brethren and sisters had not needful food; many were destitute of convenient clothing; many were out of business, and that without their own fault; and many sick and ready to perish: that I had done what in me lay to feed the hungry, to clothe the naked, to employ the poor, and to visit the sick; but was not, alone, sufficient for these things; and therefore desired all whose hearts were as my heart, 1) To bring what clothes each could spare, to be distributed among those that wanted most. 2) To give weekly a penny, or what they could afford, for the relief of the poor and sick.

My design, I told them, is to employ, for the present, all the women who are out of business, and desire it, in knitting. To these we will first give the common price for what work they do; and then add, according as they need. Twelve persons are apppointed to inspect these, and to visit and provide things needful for the sick. Each of these is to visit all the sick within their district, every other day; and to meet on Tuesday evening, to give an account of what they have done, and consult what can be done further. —John Wesley's *Journal*

8

May 8, 1705   A son born, 16th child of Samuel and Susanna Wesley, in Epworth. [See May 30]

May 8, 1706   Martha born, 17th child of Samuel and Susanna Wesley, in Epworth.

(Many Wesley birthdates are conjectural. See *The Family* at the front of the book.)

I will not forbear writing, in the midst of my best business, to one whom my soul loves, whose perfection I long for, whom I trust to meet at the marriage of the Lamb.

It would have done you good to have been with us at St. Mewan's on Monday evening, while the great congregation felt 'Th'overwhelming power of saving grace.' Next morning we were in like manner refreshed at St. Ewe. Last night at Penryn our hearts were comforted with our Lord's presence. I find my way prepared in every place, and want nothing but you to be a partaker of our joy.

Very many loving friends of yours, whom you never saw, inquire after you. By and by I shall allure you hither....This day se'nnight I expect to revisit this place. If I do not first hear from you, I question whether I shall have the heart to write again before my return to Bristol. You may suppose me something eager to know what is become of our son and heir, our sister, friends in Garth, London, Bristol, &c. What are you about? How do you go on in your family? whether my brother is come? whom have you heard at the room? what visits have you made, or received? and above all, how your own soul prospers? —Charles Wesley, a letter to his wife from Cornwall, 1753

Sarah Wesley (Mrs. Charles Wesley). Painting attributed to John Russell, R.A. She outlived her husband by 34 years and died at 96.

May

10

Your first point is to repent and believe the gospel....Let the Spirit of God bear witness with your spirit that you are a child of God, and let the love of God be shed abroad in your heart by the Holy Ghost.   —John Wesley to his nephew Samuel, Charles' son, August 1784

Samuel Wesley, son of Charles and Sarah, was an eminent musician. For periods of his life he led what seemed to the Wesleys a profligate lifestyle and his conversion to Catholicism came as a particular blow to his father. His writings show him to be thoughtful and witty.

11

May 11, 1788   Still, the more I reflect the more I am convinced that the Methodists ought not to leave the Church. I judge that to lose a thousand, yea ten thousand, of our people would be a less evil than this....Our glorying has hitherto been not to be a separate body. —John Wesley, Letter to Henry Moore

May 12, 1739   John Wesley lays the foundation stone for the New Room in the Horse Fair, Bristol. Three days earlier he wrote:

We took possession of a piece of ground, near St. James's churchyard, in the Horse Fair, where it was designed to build a room, large enough to contain both the societies of Nicholas and Baldwin Street, and such of their acquaintance as might desire to be present with them, at such times as the Scripture was expounded.   —John Wesley's *Journal*

The New Room, Bristol. The clock at left was purchased by John Wesley. The two-decker pulpit was in the fashion of Georgian England.

I have received a letter from my sister Hetty since my last to you, wherein she tells me her child is dead, and she has set up a school; by which, though not meeting with so much encouragement as she expected, she hopes to get food at least.   —Letter from Samuel, Jr., to John, May 1727

14

Those that have but little time, have still more reason to improve that little. The unprofitable servant was not condemned because he had but one talent, but for not improving it. A little time well spent is more valuable than many years or days, or hours spent in vanity. —Susanna Wesley

Charles Wesley in his middle years

15

I was glad to hear of one of our English brethren, lately brought back by a little child, who told his father something came and disturbed him so that he could not sleep at night, since they left off family prayer. —Charles Wesley's *Journal*

16

What is Christian perfection? The loving God with all our heart, mind, soul, and strength. This implies that no wrong temper, none contrary to love, remains in the soul; and that all the thoughts, words, and actions are governed by pure love. —John Wesley, *A Plain Account of Christian Perfection* [1766]

17

May 17, 1701 Unnamed twins born, 12th and 13th children of Samuel and Susanna Wesley, in Epworth. Soon die. (See note to *The Family*.)

May 18, 1699   John Wesley, 10th child, born to Samuel and Susanna Wesley at Epworth. Soon dies. In a custom common at the time, the name is used again for a later son, the John Wesley who founds Methodism.

To a Mother, on the Death of Her Children
By Mrs. Wright

Though sorer sorrows than their birth
Your children's death has given;
Mourn not that others bear for earth,
While you have peopled heaven!

If now so painful 'tis to part,
O think, that when you meet,
Well bought with shortly fleeting smart
Is never-ending sweet!

What if those little angels, nigh
T'assist your latest pain,
Should hover round you when you die,
And leave you not again?

Say, shall you then regret your woes,
Or mourn your teeming years?
One moment will reward your throes,
And overpay your tears.

Redoubled thanks will fill your song:
Transported while you view
Th'inclining, happy, infant throng,
That owe their bliss to you!*
    —Hetty Wesley Wright

How do the rays of the candle brought into the room instantly disperse into every corner? Again: here are three candles, yet there is but one light. Explain this, and I will explain the Three-One God.   —John Wesley, Sermon 55, *On the Trinity* (1775)

May 21, 1738   Charles Wesley's evangelical conversion on Whitsunday. In celebration he writes this hymn of personal experience, first published in *Hymns and Sacred Poems* in 1739.

And can it be that I should gain
An interest in the Saviour's blood?
Died He for me, who caused His pain?
For me, who Him to death pursued?
Amazing love! How can it be
That Thou, my God, shouldst die for me!

'Tis mystery all! The Immortal dies!
Who can explore His strange design?
In vain the first-born seraph tries
To sound the depths of love divine!
'Tis mercy all! let earth adore,
Let angel-minds inquire no more.

Long my imprisoned spirit lay
Fast bound in sin and nature's night;
Thine eye diffused a quickening ray,
I woke, the dungeon flamed with light;
My chains fell off, my heart was free,
I rose, went forth, and followed Thee.*
　　—Charles Wesley

Charles Wesley depicted in a stained glass window at City Road Chapel, writing his famous conversion hymn, "Where Shall My Wondering Soul Begin."

May 22, 1750 I do not think either the Church of England, or the people called Methodists, or any other particular society under heaven to be 'the true Church of Christ', for that church is but one, and contains all the true believers on earth. But I conceive every society of true believers to be a branch of the one, true, Church of Christ.   —John Wesley, Letter to Gilbert Boyce

I went to America to convert the Indians; but oh! who shall convert me? who, what is he that will deliver me from this evil heart of unbelief? I have a fair summer religion. I can talk well; nay, and believe myself, while no danger is near: but let death look me in the face, and my spirit is troubled.   —John Wesley's *Journal* February 1738

May 24, 1738   John Wesley's heart is strangely warmed at Aldersgate:

I think it was about five this morning, that I opened my Testament on those words, "There are given unto us exceeding great and precious promises, even that ye should be partakers of the divine nature" (2 Peter 1:4). Just as I went out, I opened it again on those words, "Thou art not far from the kingdom of God." In the afternoon I was asked to go to St. Paul's. The anthem was, "Out of the deep have I called unto thee, O Lord: Lord hear my voice. O let Thine ears consider well the voice of my complaint. If thou, Lord, wilt be extreme to mark what is done amiss, O Lord, who may abide it? For there is mercy with thee; therefore shalt thou be feared. O Israel, trust in the Lord: for with the Lord there is mercy, and with Him is plenteous redemption. And He shall redeem Israel from all his sins."

In the evening I went very unwillingly to a society in Aldersgate Street, where one was reading Luther's preface to the Epistle to the Romans. About a quarter before nine, while he was describing the change which God works in the heart through faith in Christ, I felt my heart strangely warmed. I felt I did trust in Christ, Christ alone, for salvation: and an assurance was given me, that He had taken away my sins, even mine, and saved me from the law of sin and death.   —John Wesley's *Journal*

Opposite page: The monument at the entrance to the Museum of London, near the site of the church in Aldersgate where John Wesley felt his heart strangely warmed. The plaque transcribes the entry cited above from his Journal.

Jesus the Savior reigns,
The God of truth and love;
When He had purged our stains,
He took His seat above.
Lift up your heart, lift up your voice;
Rejoice; again I say, Rejoice.
    —Charles Wesley, 1746

The organ from the Foundery known as Charles Wesley's organ is now at City Road Chapel.

Justification is another word for pardon. It is the forgiveness of all our sins, and (what is necessarily implied therein) our acceptance with God. The price whereby this hath been procured for us (commonly termed the 'meritorious cause' of our justification) is the blood and righteousness of Christ, or (to express it a little more clearly) all that Christ hath done and suffered for us till 'he poured out his soul for the transgressors.'   —John Wesley, Sermon 43, *The Scripture Way of Salvation* (1765)

May

27

Be gracious to my relations, to all that are endeared to me by their kindnesses or acquaintance, to all who remember me in their prayers or desire to be remembered in mine. Sanctify, O merciful Lord, the friendship which Thou hast granted me with these Thy servants. Let our prayers be heard for each other, while our hearts are united in Thy fear and love; and graciously unite them therein more and more.   —John Wesley

28

My ordinary employment, in public, was now as follows: Every morning I read prayers and preached at Newgate. Every evening I expounded a portion of Scripture at one or more of the societies. On Monday, in the afternoon, I preached abroad, near Bristol; on Tuesday, at Bath and Two-mile-hill alternately; on Wednesday, at Baptist Mills; every other Thursday, near Pensford; every other Friday, in another part of Kingswood; on Saturday, in the afternoon, and Sunday morning, in the Bowling Green (which lies near the middle of the city): on Sunday, at eleven, near Hannam Mount; at two, at Clifton; and at five on Rose Green.   —John Wesley's *Journal*

The Old Rectory, Epworth

May

May 29, 1739 Charles Wesley first engages in preaching in the fields.

Transportation was difficult in rural Britain in the 17th-18th centuries. Below: Man and horse negotiate flooded fenland similar to the countryside around Epworth in the Wesleys' time. Although Dutch engineers had been brought over to drain the land — in a move that brought both windmills and controversy over the disposition by the King of rescued land — some areas remained impassable during wet seasons. Samuel Wesley often commuted between Epworth and Wroote by boat.

Opposite page: Jonathan Spilsbury's engraved portrait of Charles Wesley. The only one published during Wesley's lifetime, it is considered to be the best likeness.

May 30, 1705   Unnamed infant born three weeks previously is smothered when the nurse rolls over on him in the night.

Be with me, O God, in a time of deep adversity, which is apt to affect my mind too much and to dispose to anxious, doubtful, and unbelieving thoughts. May I give way to no direct murmurings, no repinings at the prosperity of others, no harsh reflections on Providence, but may I maintain a constant acknowledgement of Thy justice and goodness. Save me from thinking severely or unjustly of others: from being too much dejected or disposed to peevishness, covetousness, or negligence in affairs: from working too much or too little.   —Susanna Wesley

JUNE

The Charterhouse Portrait of John Wesley, showing John at age 13, in the school uniform. By an unknown artist, it may be the artist's conception painted many years later, but is regarded as probably a good likeness.

June 1, 1760   It matters not how long we live, but how well.   —John Wesley, Letter to Dorothy Furly

1

2

Next to your wife are your children, immortal spirits whom God hath, for a time, entrusted to your care, that you may train them up in all holiness, and fit them for the enjoyment of God in eternity. This is a glorious and important trust; seeing one soul is of more value than all the world beside. Every child, therefore, you are to watch over with the utmost care, that, when you are called to give an account of each to the Father of Spirits, you may give your accounts with joy, and not with grief.
—John Wesley, from *Sermon On Family Religion*

3

There are two ways of writing or speaking to children: the one is, to let ourselves down to them; the other, to lift them up to us.   —John Wesley, Preface to *Hymns for Children* (1790)

4

June 4, 1738 The gospel is in truth but one great promise, from the beginning of it to the end.
—John Wesley's *Journal*

June 5, 1739 There was a great expectation at Bath, of what a noted man was to do to me there; and I was much entreated not to preach, because no one knew what might happen. By this report I also gained a much larger audience, among whom were many of the rich and great. I told them plainly, the Scripture had concluded them all under sin — high and low, rich and poor, one with another. Many of them seemed to be a little surprised, and were sinking apace into seriousness, when their champion appeared, and coming close to me, asked by what authority I did these things. I replied, "By the authority of Jesus Christ, conveyed to me by the (now) Archbishop of Canterbury, when he laid hands upon me, and said, 'Take thou authority to preach the gospel.'" He said, "This is contrary to Act of Parliament: this is a conventicle." I answered, "Sir, the conventicles mentioned in that Act (as the preamble shows) are seditious meetings: but this is not such; here is no shadow of sedition; therefore it is not contrary to that Act." He replied, "I say it is: and, beside, your preaching frightens people out of their wits." "Sir, did you ever

hear me preach?" "No." "How then can you judge of what you never heard?" "Sir, by common report." "Common report is not enough. Give me leave, sir, to ask, Is not your name Nash?" "My name is Nash." "Sir, I dare not judge of you by common report: I think it not enough to judge by." Here he paused a while, and, having recovered himself, said, "I desire to know what this people comes here for," on which one replied, "Sir, leave him to me: let an old woman answer him. You, Mr. Nash, take care of your body; we take care of our souls; and for the food of our souls we come here." He replied not a word, but walked away.   —John Wesley's *Journal*

6

June 6, 1742   Not permitted to preach in the Epworth church, John Wesley preaches on his father's tombstone, taking for his theme "The kingdom of heaven is not meat and drink; but righteousness, and peace, and joy in the Holy Ghost."

John Wesley preaching on his father's tomb in Epworth, to a rather distinguished company.

7

June 7, 1739   I preached at Priest Down. In the midst of the prayer after sermon, two men (hired, as we afterwards understood, for that purpose) began singing a ballad. After a few mild words (for I saw some that were angry), used without effect, we all began singing a psalm, which put them utterly to silence. We then poured out our souls in prayer for them, and they appeared altogether confounded.   —John Wesley's *Journal*

A scruple in the mind is as gravel in the shoe, it vexeth the Conscience as that hurts the foot. —Dr. Samuel Annesley

June 9, 1742   I rode over to a neighboring town, to wait upon a justice of peace, a man of candor and understanding; before whom (I was informed) their angry neighbors had carried a whole wagon-load of these new heretics. But when he asked what they had done, there was a deep silence, for that was a point their conductors had forgot. At length one said, "Why, they pretended to be better than other people; and besides, they prayed from morning to night." Mr S. asked, "But have they done nothing besides?" "Yes, sir," said an old man: "an't please your worship, they have converted my wife. Till she went among them, she had such a tongue! And now she is as quiet as a lamb." "Carry them back, carry them back," replied the justice, "and let them convert all the scolds in the town." —John Wesley's *Journal*

'John Wesley Preaching in the Open Air at Willybank' in Ireland, painted by Maria Spilsbury-Taylor. Both John and Charles visited Ireland several times.

10

Samuel Wesley, Jr., marries Ursula Berry, daughter of an Anglican vicar, in 1715. Of her he writes:

> Her hair and skin are as the berry brown;
> Soft is her smile and graceful is her frown;
> Her stature low, 'tis something less than mine;
> Her shape, though good, not exquisitely fine;
> Though round her hazel eyes some sadness lies,
> Their sprightly gladness can sometimes surprise.

11

> Unsearchable Thy judgments are,
> O Lord, a bottomless abyss!
> Yet sure, Thy love, Thy guardian care
> O'er all Thy works extended is:
> Oh! why didst Thou the blessing send?
> Or why thus snatch away my friend?
> —John Wesley, after he was prevented from marrying Grace Murray

12

> Source of Light! Thou bid'st the sun,
> On his burning axles run;
> The stars like dust around him fly,
> And strew the area of the sky....
> —Samuel Wesley

13

June 13, 1726   Charles Wesley enters Christ Church, Oxford, age 19.

14

Always take advice or reproof as a favor; it is the surest mark of love.   —John Wesley

For a Sick Child (John 4:46-53)

Jesus, great healer of mankind,
Who dost our sorrows bear,
Let an afflicted parent find
An answer to his prayer!

I look for help in Thee alone,
To Thee for succour fly;
My son is sick, my darling son,
And at the point to die!

By deep distress a suppliant made,
By agony of grief;
Most justly might Thy love upbraid
My lingering unbelief.

But Thou art ready still to run,
And grant our heart's desire:
Lord, in Thy healing power come down
Before my child expire!

Surely, if Thou pronounce the word,
If Thou the answer give,
My dying son shall be restored,
And to Thy glory live.

Rebuke the fever in this hour,
Command it to depart;
Now, let me now behold Thy power,
And give Thee all my heart!

O save the father in the son!
Restore him, Lord, to me!
My heart the miracle shall own,
And give him back to Thee.

I will, I will obey Thy word,
To Thee my all resign;
I and my house will serve the Lord,
And live forever Thine!
    —Samuel Wesley, Jr., from *Poems on Several
    Occasions*

16

June 16, 1734   I am as indifferent as it is lawful for any person to be whether I ever change my state or not, because I think a single life is the more excellent way; and there are also several reasons why I rather desire to continue as I am. One is, because I desire to be entirely disengaged from the world; but the chief is, I am so well apprised of the great duty a wife owes to her husband, that I think it almost impossible she should ever discharge it as she ought. But I can scarce say that I have the liberty of choosing, for my relations are continually soliciting me to marry.   —Kezzy Wesley to her brother John

17

June 17, 1703   John Wesley born, 14th or 15th child of Samuel and Susanna Wesley, in Epworth. [Note that in 1752 England accepted the Gregorian calendar, which meant that the eleven days between September 2 and 14 were removed from the calendar. In following the logic of this, Wesley moved his birthday from the 17th of June to the 28th. Hence, his annual self-examination falls on the latter date.]

The baptismal font in St. Andrew's parish church in Epworth, where John and many of his siblings were baptised.

18

No wise parent should suffer a child to drink any tea (or at least, till it is ten or twelve years old) or to taste spice or sugar. Milk, milk-porridge, and water-gruel are the proper breakfast for children. Washing the head every morning in cold water prevents rheums, and cures coughs, old headaches, and sore eyes. —John Wesley, *Primitive Physic*

19 June 19, 1771 When I was much younger than I am now, I thought myself almost infallible; but I bless God I know myself better now. —John Wesley, Letter to the Countess of Huntingdon, a great supporter and worker for the Methodists

20 Our children were taught as soon as they could speak the Lord's prayer, which they were made to say at rising and bedtime constantly, to which, as they grew bigger, were added a short prayer for their parents, and some collects, a short catechism, and some portion of Scripture as their memories could bear. They were very early made to distinguish the Sabbath from other days, before they could well speak or go. They were as soon taught to be still at family prayers, and to ask a blessing immediately after, which they used to do by signs, before they could kneel or speak. —Susanna Wesley

21 I humbly and heartily thank Thee for all the favors Thou hast bestowed on me: for creating me after Thine own image, for daily preserving me by Thy good providence, for redeeming me by the death of Thy blessed Son, and for the assistance of Thy Holy Spirit; for causing me to be born in a Christian country, for blessing me with plentiful means of salvation, with religious parents and friends, and frequent returns of thy ever blessed sacrament. I also thank Thee for Thy temporal blessings; for the preservation of me this night, for my health, strength, food, raiment, and all the other comforts and necessities of life. —John Wesley

22 Let everyone enjoy the present hour. —Susanna Wesley

Susanna Annesley Wesley, from a portrait which hangs in the Old Rectory, Epworth.

23

June 23, 1705   Samuel Wesley arrested for debts and imprisoned at Lincoln Castle. From prison he writes:

I don't despair of doing some good here (and so I sha'n't quite lose the end of living), and it may be, do more in this new parish than in my old one: for I have leave to read prayers every morning and afternoon here in the prison, and to preach once a Sunday, which I choose to do in the afternoon when there is no sermon at the minster. And I'm getting acquainted with my brother jail-birds as fast as I can; and shall write to London next post, to the Society for propagating Christian Knowledge, who, I hope, will send me some books to distribute among them.

24

June 24, 1720   John Wesley enters Christ Church, Oxford, age 17.

25

June 25, 1744   First Methodist Conference gathers in London.

Give me one hundred preachers who fear nothing but sin and desire nothing but God, and I care not a straw whether they be clergymen or laymen, such alone will shake the gates of hell and set up the kingdom of Heaven on earth....

The five following days we spent in conference with many of our brethren (come from several parts), who desire nothing but to save their own souls and those that hear them.   —John Wesley's *Journal*

26

June 26, 1739   I preached near the house we had a few days before begun to build for a school, in the middle of Kingswood, near a little sycamore tree, during a violent storm of rain, on those words: "As the rain cometh down from heaven, and returned not thither, but watereth the earth, and maketh it bring forth and bud: so shall My word be..."   —John Wesley's *Journal*

27

Let's make it our business to be as much Ministers out of the Pulpit as in it. The well discharge of the Ministry is an intolerable drudgery to a carnal heart: to have not our Sermons, but our occasional discourses; to have not only our words, but our silence speak us Ministers of Christ; to be always upon our watch (if I may so speak) sleeping and waking, that is, to sleep no more than is necessary to our watchfulness; who that is not gracious (I had almost said) eminently gracious, can endure it?
—Dr. Samuel Annesley

June

28

June 28, 1703   John Wesley's "adopted" birthday [see June 17]

June 28, 1774   This being my birthday, the first day of my seventy-second year, I was considering, How is this, that I find just the same strength as I did thirty years ago? That my sight is considerably better now, and my nerves firmer, than they were then? That I have none of the infirmities of old age, and have lost several I had in my youth? The grand cause is, the good pleasure of God, who doeth whatsoever pleaseth Him. The chief means are: 1. My constantly rising at four, for about fifty years. 2. My generally preaching at five in the morning; one of the most healthy exercises in the world. 3. My never travelling less, by sea or land, than four thousand five hundred miles in a year.

Detail of the statue of John Wesley behind the New Room, Bristol. Until recently, this was the only male equestrian statue in Great Britain of someone not a soldier.

I am seventy-three years old, and far abler to preach than I was at three-and-twenty. What natural means has God used to produce so wonderful an effect? 1. Continual exercise and change of air, by travelling above four thousand miles in a year. 2. Constant rising at four. 3. The ability, if ever I want, to sleep immediately. 4. The never losing a night's sleep in my life. 5. Two violent fevers, and two deep consumptions. These, it is true, were rough medicines: but they were of admirable service; causing my flesh to come again as the flesh of a little child. May I add, lastly, evenness of temper? I *feel* and *grieve*; but, by the grace of God, I *fret* at nothing. But still "the help that is done upon earth, He doeth it Himself." And this He doeth in answer to many prayers. —John Wesley's *Journal,* June 28, 1776

God grant I may never live to be useless!   —John Wesley's *Journal,* June 28, 1783

Above: One of John Wesley's lanterns.
Opposite page: The old school at Kingswood. Engraving by James Heath, published in 1790. The second figure from the left in the foreground is John Wesley.

At the end of 1739, John Wesley wrote in his *Journal:* Kingswood does not now, as a year ago, resound with cursing and blasphemy, it is no more filled with drunkenness and uncleanness, and the idle diversions that naturally lead thereto. It is no longer full of wars and fightings, of clamor and bitterness, of wrath and envyings. Peace and love are there.

That their children, too, might know the things which make for their peace, it was some time since proposed to build a house in Kingswood; in June last the foundation was laid. The ground made choice of was in the middle of the wood, between the London and Bath roads, not far from that called Two-mile-hill, about three measured miles from Bristol.

Here a large room was begun for the school, having four small rooms at either end for the schoolmasters (and, perhaps, if it should please God, some poor children) to lodge in. Two persons are ready to teach, so soon as the house is fit to receive them.   —John Wesley's *Journal*

June

JULY

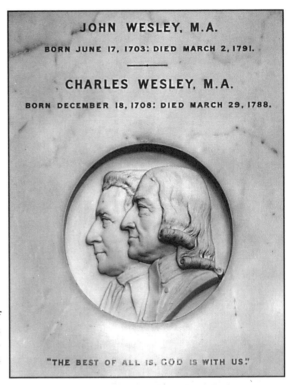

JOHN WESLEY, M.A.

BORN JUNE 17, 1703: DIED MARCH 2, 1791.

CHARLES WESLEY, M.A.

BORN DECEMBER 18, 1708: DIED MARCH 29, 1788.

"THE BEST OF ALL IS, GOD IS WITH US."

Marble relief of Charles and John Wesley on the monument to them in Westminster Abbey

July 1, 1741   I do indeed rejoice in my Sons, and am much pleas'd that they have in any means been service-able to your Ladyship. You'll pardon the fondness of a mother if I exceed in commending them, but I've known few (if any) that have labored more diligently and unweariedly in the Service of our Dear Lord: and blessed be His Great Name, He hath set His seal to their ministry and hath made them instrumental in bringing many lowly to God. And though in the eye of the world they appear despicable, men of no estate or figure, and daily suffer contempt, reproach and shame among men, yet to me they appear more honorable than they would do if the one were Archbishop of Canterbury and the other of York.   —Susanna Wesley

1

2

Be pleased, O Lord, to take me, with my parents, my friends and relations, and my enemies, into Thy almighty protection this night. Refresh me with such comfortable rest that I may rise more fit for Thy service. Let me lie down with holy thoughts of Thee, and when I wake, let me be still present with Thee.   —John Wesley

3

July 3, 1731
Dear Mother,
I heartily thank you for your kind letter: when this bitterness will be over with my wife I cannot tell. Her Body is so weak that the Mind must of necessity be influenced by it. I for my part entirely join with you in your belief that my boy died in the best time, for him at least.   —Samuel, Jr.

4

July 4, 1745   Where there is no liberty there can be no moral good or evil, no virtue or vice....There is no virtue but where an intelligent being knows, loves, and chooses what is good; nor is there any vice but where such a being knows, loves, and chooses what is evil.   —John Wesley, Sermon 62, *The End of Christ's Coming* (1781)

5

O Father, King! whose Heavenly face
Shines serene on all Thy race;
We Thy magnificence adore,
And Thy well-known aid implore:
Nor vainly for Thy help we call;
Nor can we want, for Thou art All!
   —Samuel Wesley, from *Eupolis's Hymn to the Creator.* The Epworth rector was rated one of the better minor poets of his time. Scholars think that daughter Hetty may have helped to write this particular poem.

Religion is not to be confined to the church or closet, nor exercised only in prayer and meditation, but everywhere I am in His presence.   —Susanna Wesley

6

You are a Christian minister, speaking and writing to save souls. Have this end always in your eye, and you will never designedly use an hard word. Use all the sense, learning, and fire you have; forgetting yourself, and remembering only these are the souls for whom Christ died; heirs of an happy or miserable eternity. —John Wesley, Letter to Samuel Furly

7

I thought I might live in a more exemplary manner in some things. I might pray more for the people, and speak with more warmth to those with whom I have an opportunity of conversing.   —Susanna Wesley, Letter to Samuel

8

This engraving by T.A. Dean, often presented as Susanna Wesley, is now believed to be a portrait of Lady Rudd, Charles Wesley's sister-in-law.

Consult duty not events. There's nothing in the world for us to do but to mind our duty.   —Dr. Samuel Annesley

9

The best preparation I know of for suffering is a regular and exact performance of present duty.   —Susanna Wesley

10

July

11

July 11, 1778   O praise God for all you have, and trust Him for all you want!   —John Wesley, Letter to Alexander Knox

12

July 12, 1791   Martha Wesley Hall dies and is interred with her brother John at City Road Chapel. Her obituary notice in *The Gentleman's Magazine* says "She was equally distinguished by piety, understanding, and sweetness of temper. Her sympathy for the wretched, and her bounty, even to the worthless, will eternise her memory in better worlds than this."

Her niece Sarah had asked to be with her at the end. "Yes, you may be with me if you are able to bear it; but I charge you not to grieve for me more than half an hour." Sarah records the scene:

"Blessed be His name," she replied, "I do not *tremble;* He does not cause me to tremble. After some pause, she broke out, "My *dear* Girl, to *Him* I commend *you!* God be merciful to us both!"...

I said when the poor Body is thus become unfit for its inhabitant and the spirit weigh'd down with weakness and infirmities, this calmness, this composure is Triumph. My dearest Aunt, if I a poor feeble Creature feel such love toward you, what must be that of our dear Lord!

Then looking upwards with an energy plainly indicating a view of the invisible world, she asked me if I saw that Star — and raising up her dying hands, bid me *"SHOUT!"* She spoke no more, and the happy spirit passed so easily we could not ascertain the moment of its flight. At 10 past 8 she was gone.

I preached [yesterday] at Newgate to the condemned felons, and visited one of them in his cell, sick of the fever; a poor black that had robbed his master. I told him of one who came down from heaven to save lost sinners, and him in particular; described the sufferings of the Son of God, His sorrows, agony and death. He listened with all the signs of eager astonishment. I left him waiting for the salvation of God.

[This morning] at half-hour past nine their irons were knocked off, and their hands tied. I went in a coach with Sparks, Washington, and a friend of Newington's. By half-hour past ten we came to Tyburn, waited till eleven: then were brought the children appointed to die. I got upon the cart with Sparks and Broughton....I prayed first, then Sparks and Broughton....The black had spied me coming out of the coach, and saluted me with his looks. As often as his eyes met mine, he smiled.
—Charles Wesley's *Journal*

What will the consequence be...if family religion be neglected?... if care be not taken of the rising generation? Will not the present revival of religion in a short time die away?   —John Wesley

July 15, 1764   Order is Heaven's first Law.   —Martha Wesley

John Wesley's spurs

July

16

July 16, 1790 For upward to eighty-six years I have kept my accounts exactly. I will not attempt it any longer, being satisfied with the continual conviction that I save all I can, and give all I can, that is, all I have.
—John Wesley's *Journal*

17

July 17, 1739 I went to a gentleman in the town [Bradford], who had been present when I preached at Bath, and, with the strongest marks of sincerity and affection, wished me good luck in the name of the Lord. But it was past. I found him now quite cold. He began disputing on several heads; and at last told me plainly, one of our own college had informed him they always took me to be a little crack-brained at Oxford.   —John Wesley's *Journal*

18

Anacreontics — To My Wife
Ere I found you fair and good;
Ere the nut-brown maid I view'd;
Sunny walks and spreading trees
Sports and theatres could please.
Soon as e'er my Love was known,
All I left for her alone.*
—Samuel Wesley, Jr.

19

July 19, 1761 I hastened back to the love-feast at Birstal. It was the first of the kind which had been there. Many were surprised when I told them, "The very design of a love-feast is a free and familiar conversation, in which every man, yea, and woman has liberty to speak whatever may be to the glory of God." Several then did speak, and not in vain: the flame ran from heart to heart.
—John Wesley's *Journal*

July 20, 1742   I found my mother on the borders of eternity. But she had no doubt or fear; nor any desire but (as soon as God should call) 'to depart and to be with Christ.'   —John Wesley's *Journal*

And at what time soever a sinner thus believes, be it in early childhood, in the strength of his years, or when he is old and hoary-haired, God justifieth that ungodly one; God for the sake of his Son pardoneth and absolveth him who had in him till then no good thing.   —John Wesley, Sermon, *Justification by Faith* (1746)

July 22, 1779   I took coach for London. I was nobly attended: behind the coach were ten convicted felons, loudly blaspheming and rattling their chains; by my side sat a man with a loaded blunderbuss, and another upon the coach.   —John Wesley's *Journal*

Inscription on the monument to Susanna at City Road Chapel, London

23

July 23, 1742   Susanna Wesley dies, City Road, London, age 73.

About three in the afternoon I went to my mother, and found her change was near. I sat down on the bedside. She was in her last conflict; unable to speak, but I believe quite sensible. Her look was calm and serene, and her eyes fixed upward, while we commended her soul to God. From three to four the silver cord was loosing, and the wheel breaking at the cistern; and then without any struggle, or sigh, or groan, the soul was set at liberty. We stood round the bed and fulfilled her last request, uttered a little before she lost her speech: "Children, as soon as I am released, sing a psalm of praise to God." —John Wesley's *Journal*   Those present include all five surviving daughters (Emilia, Susanna, Anne, Mehetabel, Martha); Charles was out of the city.

24

July 24, 1800   You guessed right, that your brother Charles had paid his usual respects at Windsor. He and I wished for your company...We went to the castle on our way to the chapel. Your brother left us to wait at the Lodge, where he met the King, who immediately noticed him and said he should see him to play in the evening on his own organ which he thought a better one than St. George's. However, Charles pleased him much in playing there "Unto us a Son is Born" and the "Hallelujah Chorus" which his majesty desired....

His Majesty being told who I was, came into the room to speak to me, and asked me some questions about my children's genius for music and your father's liking it. He said he thought it was intended for the noblest purposes. I added my opinion, that I believed it was to raise our hearts above this world. His opinion of Handel's *Messiah* was higher than he chose to say.

My son's appointment of organist to his Royal Majesty is only Honorary at present, but we must wait with patience and trust Providence will order all things for the best.   —Sarah Wesley, Charles' widow, to their daughter Sally

25

For one seemingly kill'd with Lightning, or a Damp, or suffocated: Plunge him immediately into cold water; or, Blow strongly with bellows down his throat: This may recover a person seemingly drowned.   —John Wesley, *Primitive Physic*

26

July 26, 1736   Charles Wesley leaves Georgia to return to England [lands December 3].

27

Our Lord knew what was in men when he directed us to pray, "Lead us not into temptation."   —Susanna Wesley

28

July 28, 1746   I began my week's experiment of leaving off tea; but my flesh protested against it. I was but half awake and half alive all day; and my headache so increased toward noon that I could neither speak nor think.   —Charles Wesley's *Journal*

29

[At Chester] I met with one of the most extraordinary phenomena that I ever saw, or heard of:—Mr. Sellars has in his yard a large Newfoundland dog, and an old raven. These have fallen deeply in love with each other and never desire to be apart. The bird has learned the bark of the dog, so that few can distinguish them. She is inconsolable when he goes out; and if he stays out a day or two, she will get up all the bones and scraps she can, and hoard them up for him till he comes back.   —John Wesley's *Journal*

Opposite page: Charles Wesley as a young man. Attributed to Henry Hudson.

July

30

John Whitelamb, widower of Mary Wesley, dies in July 1769 (date unknown). His epitaph in Wroote graveyard reads: "Worthy of Imitation."

31

July 31, 1744   I rode to St. Just. I climbed up and down Cape Cornwall with my brother Meriton, to the needless hazard of our necks. I preached in the afternoon to a larger congregation than ever, and continued my discourse till night, from Luke xxi 34. The Spirit of love was poured out abundantly, and great grace was upon all. I walked to the Society; stood upon the hill, and sang, and prayed, and rejoiced with exceeding great joy. I concluded the day and month as I would wish to conclude my life.   —Charles Wesley's *Journal*

AUGUST

Gravestone marking Susanna Wesley's burial place in Bunhill Fields across from City Road Chapel in London

August 1, 1742 Almost an innumerable company of people being gathered together, about five in the afternoon, I committed to the earth the body of my mother to sleep with her fathers....I cannot but further observe, that even she (as well as her father, and grandfather, her husband, and her three sons) had been, in her measure and degree, a preacher of righteousness. —John Wesley's *Journal*

I thank Thee, O God, because in the whole course of my life there have been more mercies than afflictions and much more pleasure than pain. Though I have suffered pain and bodily infirmities, I have likewise enjoyed great intervals of rest and ease. But all my sufferings, by the admirable management of Thine omnipotent goodness, have concurred to promote my spiritual and eternal good. If, owing to the perverseness of my own will, my frequent lapses into present things and my unfaithfulness to Thy good Spirit, I have failed to reap that advantage of life's adversities which I might have done, I thank Thee because, notwithstanding all my prevarications and all the stupid opposition I have made, Thou hast never totally abandoned me. Glory be to Thee, O Lord! Amen. —Susanna Wesley, *Meditations*

Susanna Wesley's needlework case

Jesus, Lover of my soul,
Let me to Thy bosom fly,
While the nearer waters roll,
While the tempest still is nigh:
Hide me, O my Saviour, hide,
Till the storm of life be past;
Safe into the haven guide,
O receive my soul at last.*
    —Charles Wesley

August 4, 1769   John Wesley makes the first appointment of preachers to America

August 4, 1740
Dear Brother,
I should sooner have writ to you had I known where to find you, your last being dated from Oxford, and you then was going to leave that place but my Mother telling me that you are with her, I resolved speedily to write that I may get information from your own self of some things of which I know not what to think till more light be granted me.

The Methodists make a mighty noise in the nation. Most people condemn their doctrines, yet whether out of curiosity or goodness, I can't tell.   Never were any preachers more followed. Mr. Rogers and Mr. Ingam at Nottingham preached lately to upward of 10,000 souls. Now as you are the head of those people, prithee solve me a few scruples concerning them, and assure yourself I am as unprejudiced as your heart can wish and first I begin with your doctrines, as far as I know them, and then shall secondly consider your practice.

First I am informed you hold the absolute necessity of Faith before we can be justified or in any state of regeneration. Now if actual Faith be necessary to our being in a state of Salvation, to what purpose is infant Baptism? or what becomes of those who die before they come to an age capable of believing? as thousands do every year.

Now for your practice, all you Methodist preachers are regular clergymen (I think) and therefore authorised by Christ to preach the gospel, but why do you take so extraordinary a way? Why do you leave our churches to preach in fields and markets and what is become of our excellent liturgy, which cannot be used in such places?...Our clergy generally speaking are unworthy of the sacred office they hold, and if God have raised you up to reform the nation, I heartily wish you prosperity. I believe all the Methodists to be good Christians, though not infallible. May the spirit of Truth (who alone is so) guide us into all truth. I am dear Brother
Your most affectionate sister,
Emilia Harper

August

5

We are always open to instruction, willing to be wiser every day than we were before, and to change whatever we can change for the better.　—John Wesley, *A Plain Account of the People Called Methodists* (1749)

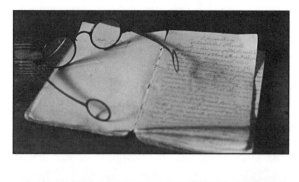

John Wesley's spectacles, placed on one of his manuscripts. Below, a tea cup, saucer and servers used by John Wesley.　These items are preserved in the Museum of Methodism at City Road Chapel.

6

A Methodist is one who has 'the love of God shed abroad in his heart by the Holy Ghost given unto him;' one who 'loves the Lord his God with all his heart, and with all his soul, and with all his mind, and with all his strength'. God is the joy of his heart, and the desire of his soul. —John Wesley, *The Character of a Methodist* (1742)

Wear no gold (whatever officers of state may do; or magistrates, as the ensign of their office), no pearls, or precious stones; use no curling of hair, or costly apparel, how grave soever....Buy no velvets, no silks, no fine linen, no superfluities, no more ornaments, though ever so much in fashion. Wear nothing, though you have it already, which is of a glaring color, or which is in any kind gay, glistening, or showy; nothing made in the very height of the fashion, nothing apt to attract the eyes of the bystanders. I do not advise women to wear rings, earrings, necklaces, lace (of whatever kind or color), or ruffles, which, little by little, may easily shoot out from one to twelve inches deep. Neither do I advise men to wear colored waistcoats, shining stockings, glittering or costly buckles or buttons, either on their coats or in their sleeves, any more than gay, fashionable, or expensive perukes....

If those who do observe [these rules] employ the money they thus save in the most excellent manner, then a part of what before only served to fat a few rich tradesmen for hell will suffice to feed and clothe and employ many more poor that seek the kingdom of heaven. —John Wesley, *Advice to the People Called Methodists, with Regard to Dress*

August 8, 1779 I was at West Street in the morning, and at the new chapel in the evening, when I took a solemn leave of the affectionate congregation. This was the last night which I spent at the Foundery. What hath God wrought there in one-and-forty years. —John Wesley's *Journal* [He moves into the new house in City Road in October.]

The Chapel at West Street, for years a center of the Methodist Societies in London.

August

9

The plaque marking the site of the Foundery, on Tabernacle Street near City Road Chapel in London.

10

August 10, 1775   It is not safe to live or die without love.
—John Wesley, Letter to Charles Wesley

11

The love of God, as it is the sovereign remedy of all miseries, so in particular it effectually prevents all the bodily disorders the passions introduce, by keeping the passions themselves within due bounds. And by the unspeakable joy, and perfect calm, serenity, and tranquility it gives the mind, it becomes the most powerful of all the means of health and long life.   —John Wesley, Preface to *Primitive Physic*

12

August 12, 1767   I took coach. The next day we reached Grantham, and London about seven on Friday evening; having run, that day, an hundred and ten miles. On the road I read over Seller's *History of Palmyra* and Norden's *Travels into Egypt and Abyssinia*; two as dry and unsatisfying books as ever I read in my life.   —John Wesley's *Journal*

13

Cure for The Lethargy: Snuff strong vinegar up the nose. —John Wesley, *Primitive Physic*

14

As a very little dust will disorder a clock, and the least sand will obscure our sight, so the least grain of sin which is upon the heart will hinder its right motion toward God. —John Wesley, *A Plain Account of Christian Perfection* (1766)

15

Never correct your children to satisfy your passions, but from a sense of your duty to reclaim them from their errors, and to preserve your authority. And then be exceedingly careful to let the measure of your correction be proportionable to the fault, make great allowances for the weakness of their reason and immaturity of their judgment, but never spare them through foolish fondness when they sin against God. Instruct them in their duty and reason with them upon the several branches of it. Cherish the first dawnings of sense and reason, and endeavor to instruct their minds in their early years with a sense of religion. "Train up a child in the way he should go, and when he is old he will not depart from it." —Susanna Wesley

16

Come, Father, Son, and Holy Ghost,
To whom we for our children cry;
The good desired and wanted most,
Out of Thy richest grace supply;
The sacred discipline be given,
to train and bring them up for heaven.*
    —Charles Wesley

August

17

I know, were I myself to preach one whole year in one place, I should preach both myself and most of my congregation asleep. Nor can I ever believe it was ever the will of our Lord that any congregation should have one teacher only. We have found by long and constant experience that a frequent change of teachers is best.
—John Wesley, Letter to Samuel Walker

18

Impromptu by Miss Sarah Wesley upon being told by a gentleman that "she would have been a bewitching creature if she had not been so horribly ugly":

> Malice and envy in one point agree
> That the outside is the worst part of me.
> Smart is the [censure] as it stands contest
> Bad as it is — *thy* outside is the best.

Sally Wesley, daughter of Charles and Sarah Wesley. The likeness is a detail from Claxton's painting of those present at John Wesley's death.

August 19, 1784   I feared you were not born again; and "except a man be born again," if we may credit the Son of God, "he cannot see the kingdom of heaven;" except he experience that inward change of the earthly, sensual mind, for the mind which was in Christ Jesus.   —John Wesley to his nephew Samuel, Charles' son

19

August 20, 1764   I went to Canterbury, and opened our new chapel by praching on "One thing is needful." How is it that many Protestants, even in England, do not know that no other consecration of church or chapel is allowed, much less required, in England, than the performance of public worship therein? This is the only consecration of any church in Great Britain which is necessary or even lawful....Let this be remembered by all who talk so idly of preaching in unconsecrated places!
—John Wesley's *Journal*

20

Being at Mr. Fox's society, my heart was so full that I could not confine myself to the forms of prayer which we were accustomed to use there. Neither do I purpose to be confined to them any more; but to pray indifferently, with a form or without, as I may find suitable to particular occasions.   —John Wesley's *Journal*

21

Newbiggin, Teasdale, Methodist Chapel, dates from 1759. John Wesley preached here many times. It is still in use.

August

August 22, 1773   I preached in Illogan and at Redruth; Sunday the 22nd in St. Agnes church-town, at eight; about one at Redruth; and at five in the amphitheatre at Gwennap. The people both filled it, and covered the ground round about to a considerable distance. So that, supposing the space to be four-score yards square, and to contain five person in a square yard, thre must be above two-and-thirty thousand people; the largest assembly I ever preached to. Yet I found, upon inquiry, all could hear, even to the skirts of the congregation! Perhaps the first time that a man of seventy had been heard by thirty thousand persons at once!   —John Wesley

The natural amphitheatre at Gwennap, far the finest I know in the kingdom. It is a round, green hollow, gently shelving down, about fifty feet deep; but I suppose it is two hundred across one way, and near three hundred the other.   —John Wesley

August 24, 1662 Samuel Annesley, Susanna Wesley's father, preaches his last sermon licensed in the Church of England, while serving as Vicar at St. Giles Cripplegate in London (below). As a matter of conscience, he had refused to sign the Act of Uniformity. He eventually forms a congregation at St. Helen's, Bishopsgate, where he continues as a noted pastor and scholar.

> *Description of Dr. Annesley by Daniel Defoe:*
> The Sacred Bow he so Divinely drew,
> That every shot both hit and overthrew;
> His native Candor, and familiar Stile,
> Which did so oft his Hearers Hours beguile,
> Charm'd us with Godliness, and while he spake,
> We lov'd the Doctrine for the Teacher's sake.
> While he inform'd us what his Doctrines meant,
> By dint of Practice more than Argument,
> Strange were the Charms of his Sincerity,
> Which made his Actions and his Words agree
> At such a constant and exact a rate,
> As made a Harmony we wondered at.

St. Giles, Cripplegate, London.

August

25

The smallpox has been very mortal at Epworth most of this summer. Our family have all had it besides me, and I hope God will preserve me from it, because your father can't yet very well spare money to bury me. —Susanna to John, from Wroote, 1724

26

The truth is I am hipp'd by my voyage and journey to and from Epworth last Sunday; being lamed with having my breeches too full of water, partly with a downfall from a thunder shower and partly from the wash over the boat. Yet I thank God I was able to preach here in the afternoon, and was as well this morning as ever, except a little pain and lameness, both of which I hope to wash off with a hair of the same dog this evening. —Samuel Wesley to John

27

Sunday 1710

This is the day that the Lord hath made, I will rejoice and be glad therein. Glory be to Thee Eternal Father of spirits for so kindly and mercifully indulging one day in seven to the souls Thou hast made, wherein it is their duty as well as happiness to retire from the business and hurry of a tumultuous and vexatious world, and are permitted to enjoy a more blessed Indulgence!

Oh most happy day! Lord, I can never sufficiently adore Thy infinite love and goodness in appropriating this seventh part of my time to Thy self. May these sacred moments ever be employed in Thy service! May no vain, unnecessary or unprofitable thoughts or discourse ever rob God of his due honor and praise on this day, or deprive my soul of the peculiar advantages and blessings which are to be gained by the conscientious performance of its several duties. —Susanna Wesley

August

August 28, 1748   I wonder at those who still talk so loud of the indecency of field-preaching. The highest indecency is in St. Paul's Church, when a considerable part of the congregation are asleep, or talking, or looking about, not minding a word the preacher says. —John Wesley's *Journal*

August 29, 1779   It was one of the hottest days I have known in England. The thermometer rose to 80 degrees — as high as it usually rises in Jamaica. Being desired to visit a dying man in Kingsdown, I had no time but at two o'clock. The sun shone without a cloud; so that I had a warm journey. But I was well repaid; for the poor sinner found peace. At five I preached to an immense multitude in the square; and God comforted many drooping souls.   —John Wesley's *Journal*

I take à Kempis to have been an honest, weak man, who had more zeal than knowledge, by his condemning all mirth or pleasure as sinful or useless.   —Susanna Wesley

August 31, 1784   While you help others, God will help you.   —John Wesley, Letter to Ann Bolton

Opposite page: Portrait of John Wesley by Thomas Horsley of Sutherland. Horsley was a student of Romney and this is considered an excellent likeness of Wesley. The building in the background is City Road Chapel.

August

A ballad sheet for "A New Song in Praise of Methodism" with an image of John Wesley based on the famous portrait by Nathaniel Hone.

1

September 1-2, 1784   Fifteen years after first sending preachers to America, John Wesley made his first ordinations [see September 10], sending Mr. Whatcoat and Mr. Vasey "to serve the desolate sheep in America" with Dr. Coke.

2

Forth in Thy name, O Lord, I go
My daily labor to pursue,
Thee, only Thee resolved to know
In all I think, or speak, or do.

The task Thy wisdom has assigned
O let me cheerfully fulfil,
In all my works Thy presence find,
And prove Thy acceptable will.

Thee may I set at my right hand,
Whose eyes my inmost substance see,
And labor on at Thy command,
And offer all my works to Thee.
    —Charles Wesley

High House, Weardale (1760-61), a dales chapel of Wesley vintage, enlarged in the 19th century. The Wesleys often visited and preached here.

September

September 3, 1739 I talked largely with my mother, who told me that till a short time since she had scarce heard such a thing mentioned as the having forgiveness of sins now, or God's Spirit bearing witness with our spirit: much less did she imagine that this was the common privilege of all true believers. "Therefore," said she, "I never durst ask for it myself. But two or three weeks ago, while my son Hall [husband of her daughter Martha] was pronouncing those words, in delivering the cup to me, 'The blood of our Lord Jesus Christ, which was given for thee,' the words struck through my heart, and I knew God for Christ's sake had forgiven me all my sins."

Susanna Wesley
in an engraving
by T. A. Dean.

I asked whether her father (Dr. Annesley) had not the same faith; and, whether she had not heard him preach it to others. She answered, he had it himself; and declared, a little before his death, that for more than forty years he had no darkness, no fear, no doubt at all of his being "accepted in the Beloved." But that, nevertheless, she did not remember to have heard him preach, no, not once, explicitly upon it: whence she supposed he also looked upon it as the peculiar blessing of a few; not as promised to all the people of God.   —John Wesley's *Journal*

September

4

You are no more at liberty to throw away your health than to throw away your life. —John Wesley, Letter to Ann Bolton

---

5

September 5, 1746 [John Trembath's late illness] was a second relapse into the spotted fever [meningitis], in the height of which they gave him sack, cold milk and apples, plums, as much as he could swallow. I can see no way to account for his recovery but that he had not then finished his work. —John Wesley's *Journal*

6

September 6, 1762 A flame was kindled almost as soon as I began to speak, which increased more and more all the time I was preaching as well as during the meeting of the society. —John Wesley's *Journal*

7

A charge to keep I have,
A God to glorify,
A never-dying soul to save,
And fit it for the sky.*
—Charles Wesley

8

Wedgwood produced the Wesley teapot, so called because it features the grace John Wesley used. Thousands of these were sold. This one is Wesley's own, preserved at City Road.

September 9 to March 20, 1747-8   Charles Wesley's first visit to Ireland

9

September 9, 1766   In riding to St. Ives I called on one with whom I used to lodge two or three and twenty years ago, Alice Daniel, at Rosemergy. Her sons are all gone from her, and she has but one daughter left, who is always ill. Her husband is dead; and she can no longer read her Bible, for she is stone blind. Yet she murmurs at nothing, but cheerfully waits till her appointed time shall come. How many of these jewels may lie hid, up and down, forgotten of men, but precious in the sight of God!
—John Wesley's *Journal*

10

September 10, 1784   Letter from John Wesley to Dr. Coke, Mr. Asbury, and Our Brethren in North America, dated from Bristol

1. By a very uncommon train of providences, many of the provinces of North America are totally disjoined from their mother-country, and erected into independent States. The English Government has no authority over them, either civil or ecclesiastical, any more than over the States of Holland. A civil authority is exercised over them, partly by the Congress, partly by the provincial Assemblies. But no one either exercises or claims any ecclesiastical authority at all. In this peculiar situation some thousands of the inhabitants of these States desire my advice; and in compliance with their desire, I have drawn up a little sketch.

2. Lord King's "Account of the Primitive church" convinced me many years ago, that Bishops and Presbyters are the same order, and consequently have the same right to ordain. For many years I have been importuned, from time to time, to exercise this right, by ordaining part of our Travelling Preachers. But I have still refused, not only for peace' sake, but because I was determined as little as possible to violate the established order of the national Church to which I belonged.

September

3. But the case is widely different between England and North America. Here there are Bishops who have a legal jurisdiction: In America there are none, neither any parish Ministers. So that for some hundred miles together, there is none either to baptize, or to administer the Lord's supper. Here, therefore, my scruples are at an end; and I conceive myself at full liberty, as I violate no order, and invade no man's right, by appointing and sending laborers into the harvest.

4. I have accordingly appointed Dr. Coke and Mr. Francis Asbury to be joint Superintendents over our brethren in North America; as also Richard Whatcoat and Thomas Vasey to act as Elders among them, by baptizing and administering the Lord's supper. And I have prepared a Liturgy, little differing from that of the Church of England (I think, the best constituted national Church in the world), which I advise all the Travelling Preachers to use on the Lord's day, in all the congregations, reading the Litany only on Wednesdays and Fridays, and praying extempore on all other days. I also advise the Elders to administer the supper of the Lord on every Lord's day.

The Stable Yard at The New Room, Bristol, showing the Preachers' Stable

5. If any one will point out a more rational and scriptural way of feeding and guiding those poor sheep in the wilderness, I will gladly embrace it. At present, I cannot see any better method than that I have taken.

6. It has, indeed, been proposed to desire the English Bishops to ordain part of our Preachers for America. But to this I object. (1.) I desired the Bishop of London to ordain only one; but could not prevail. (2.) If they consented, we know the slowness of their proceedings; but the matter admits of no delay. (3.) If they would ordain them now, they would likewise expect to govern them. And how grievously would this entangle us! (4.) As our American brethren are now totally disentangled both from the State and from the English hierarchy, we dare not entangle them again, either with the one or the other. They are now at full liberty, simply to follow the Scriptures and the primitive church. And we judge it best that they should stand fast in that liberty where-with God has so strangely made them free.

11

I had had for some time a great desire to go and publish the love of God our Savior, if it were but for one day, in the Isles of Scilly....This evening three of our brethren came and offered to carry me thither if I could procure the mayor's boat, which, they said, was the best sailer of any in the town. So the next morning...John Nelson, Mr. Shepherd, and I, with three men and a pilot, sailed from St. Ives. It seemed strange to me to attempt going, in a fisher-boat, fifteen leagues upon the main ocean; especially when the waves began to swell, and hang over our heads. —John Wesley's *Journal,* 1743

In a storm off St. Ives

September

12

September 12, 1705   Samuel Wesley writes to the Archbishop of York from prison in Lincoln Castle, where he was incarcerated for not paying debts:

The other matter is concerning the stabbing of my cows in the night since I came hither, but a few weeks ago; and endeavoring thereby to starve my forlorn family in my absence; my cows being all dried by it, which was their chief subsistence; though I hope they had not the power to kill any of them outright.

The same night the iron latch of my door was twined off, and the wood hacked in order to shoot back the lock, which nobody will think was with an intention to rob my family. My housedog, who made a huge noise within doors, was sufficiently punished for his want of politics and *moderation,* for the next day but one his leg was almost chopped off by an unknown hand. 'Tis not every one could bear these things; but, I bless God, my wife is less concerned with suffering them than I am in the writing...

Most of my friends advise me to leave Epworth, if e'er I should get from hence. I confess I am not of that mind, because I may yet do good there; and 'tis like a coward to desert my post because the enemy fire thick upon me. They have only wounded me yet, and, I believe, *can't* kill me. I hope to be home by Xmass [sic]. God help my poor family!   —Samuel Wesley

13

September 13, 1735   Martha Wesley marries Westley Hall, a minister who proves unfaithful both to God and to his wife. For the first few years, however, and especially after Samuel Wesley's death, they offer a home to members of the Wesley family, particularly Susanna and Kezzy. They have ten children, most of whom die in infancy. One boy, much cared for by his uncles John and Charles, lives to the age of 14, when he dies of smallpox.

Behold the Savior of mankind
Nailed to the shameful tree!
How vast the love that Him inclined
To bleed and die for thee!

'Tis done! the precious ransom's paid!
"Receive my soul!" he cries;
See where He bows His sacred head!
He bows His head and dies.

But soon He'll break death's envious chain,
And in full glory shine;
O Lamb of God, was ever pain,
Was ever love, like Thine?
 —Samuel Wesley

Your first business is the grammar, your second finishing lessons. Your kite does not come [before] your study. —Charles Wesley writing home to his son Samuel in Bristol. (Dates of residency on the plaque on the house may prove incorrect.)

I've read the plays you sent Sister [Anne] Lambert several times, for 'tis a great pleasure to me to read a good play, though I've the same fate in that as in most other things I like, I have 'em very seldom....
Your Sincere Friend,
and Loving Sister,
Martha Wesley
[to her brother Jack]

September

17

When the house was rebuilt and the children all brought home, we entered on a strict reform; and then was begun the system of singing psalms at beginning and leaving school, morning and evening. Then also that of a general retirement at five o'clock was entered upon, when the eldest took the youngest that could speak, and the second the next, to whom they read the psalms for the day and a chapter in the New Testament; as in the morning they were directed to read the psalms and a chapter in the Old Testament, after which they went to their private prayers, before they got their breakfast or came into the family.   —Susanna Wesley

18

Grant that I may assist all my brethren with my prayers where I cannot reach them with actual services. Make me zealous to embrace all occasions that may minister to their happiness. Let Thy love to me be the pattern of my love to them.   —John Wesley

John Wesley portrait by Nathaniel Hone, 1766.

September 19, 1725   John Wesley, age 22, ordained deacon by Dr. John Potter, Bishop of Oxford, in Christ Church Cathedral

September 19, 1769 [at Bradford]   The beasts of the people were tolerably quiet till I had nearly finished my sermon. They then lifted up their voice, especially one, called a gentleman, who had filled his pocket with rotten eggs: but, a young man coming unawares clapped his hands on each side, and mashed them all at once. In an instant he was perfume all over; though it was not so sweet as balsam.   —John Wesley's *Journal*

The statue of John Wesley near St. Paul's in London. It is a direct copy from the statue in Westminster Central Hall sculpted by Samuel Manning in 1849. The inscription below identifies him as the Father of Methodism and as "Priest, Poet, Teacher of the Faith."

Every wise man therefore will allow others the same liberty of thinking which he desires they should allow him; and will no more insist on their embracing his opinions than he would have them to insist on his embracing theirs. He bears with those who differ from him, and only asks him with whom he desires to unite in love that single question. 'Is thine heart right, as my heart is with thy heart?' —John Wesley, Sermon 39, *Catholic Spirit* (1750)

September

21

September 21, 1735   Charles Wesley ordained deacon

To serve the present age,
My calling to fulfill:
O may it all my powers engage
To do my Master's will.

Help me to watch and pray,
And on Thyself rely,
Assured, if I my trust betray,
I shall for ever die.
    —Charles Wesley

22

September 22, 1728   John Wesley ordained priest

23

September 23, 1738   I was enabled to speak strong words both at Newgate and at Mr. E.'s society; and the next day at St. Anne's, and twice at St. John's, Clerkenwell; so that I fear they will bear me there no longer.   —John Wesley's *Journal*

24

Charles Wesley Jr., son of Charles and Sarah. Kelway, the organist at St. Martin in the Fields who taught him free for two years, said Charles was "the greatest genius in music I ever met with." In line more than once for outstanding positions, he found his Wesley name unpopular with high church leaders. King George III, who favored him, was overtaken by madness before he could keep promises of royal appointments.

That no girl be taught to work till she can read very well; and that she be kept to her work with the same application and for the same time that she was held to in reading. This rule also is much to be observed, for the putting young children to learn sewing before they can read perfectly is the very reason why so few women can read fit to be heard, and never to be well understood.
—Susanna Wesley

Let all you that have it in your power assert the right which the God of nature has given you. Yield not to that vile bondage any longer. You, as well as men, are rational creatures. You, like them, were made in the image of God: you are equally candidates for immortality. You too are called of God, as you have time, to 'do good unto all men.' —John Wesley, Sermon 98, *On Visiting the Sick* (1786), addressing women

It is a great thing to seize and improve the *very now*.
—John Wesley, Letter to Mary Bishop

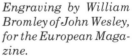

Engraving by William Bromley of John Wesley, for the European Magazine.

September

Susanna Wesley in a color portrait purported to have been found in Lincolnshire. Its whereabouts is now unknown.

---

28   September 28, 1735   Charles Wesley ordained priest

---

29   For the Head-ache: Rub the head for a quarter of an hour.

For a Chronical Head-ache: Keep your feet in warm water, a quarter of hour before you go to bed for two or three weeks. Or, wear hemlock leaves under the feet, changing them daily. Or, order a tea-kettle of cold water to be poured on your head every morning in a slender stream.   —John Wesley, *Primitive Physic*

---

30   September 30, 1785   I had a long conversation with John McGeary, one of our American preachers, just come to England. He gave a pleasing account of the work of God there, continually increasing, and vehemently importuned me to pay one more visit to America before I die. Nay, I shall pay no more visits to new worlds, till I go to the world of spirits.   —John Wesley's *Journal*

OCTOBER

The "new house" in City Road, London, where John Wesley spent his last twelve years.

It is the duty of every Christian to receive the Lord's Supper as often as he can. —John Wesley, Sermon 101, *The Duty of Constant Communion* (1787)

1

October 2, 1764 I breakfasted at the Devizes, with Mr. B..., a black swan: an honest lawyer! —John Wesley's *Journal*

2

3

October 3, 1783 It is the glory of the people called Methodists that they condemn none for their opinions or modes of worship. They think and let think, and insist upon nothing but faith working by love.   —John Wesley, Letter to Mrs. Howton

4

The kitchen in Epworth, where, according to their mother, the children "were never suffered to choose their meat, but always made to eat such things as were provided for the family.... Whatever they had, they were never permitted at those meals to eat of more than one thing, and of that sparingly enough. Drinking or eating between meals was never allowed, unless in case of sickness."

5

I magnify Thee for granting me to be born in Thy Church and of religious parents; for washing me in Thy baptism and instructing me in thy doctrine of truth and holiness; for sustaining me by Thy gracious providence and guiding me by Thy blessed Spirit; and for so often feeding my soul with Thy most precious body and blood.   —John Wesley

Written before preaching at Portland, where he saw quarrymen working the quarries from which some years before came stone for Christopher Wren's St. Paul's Cathedral

> **Come, O thou all-victorious Lord,**
> Thy power to us make known;
> Strike with the hammer of Thy word,
> And break these hearts of stone.
> O that we all might now begin
> Our foolishness to mourn,
> And turn at once from every sin,
> And to our Saviour turn!*
> —Charles Wesley

October 7, 1790   John Wesley preaches his last open-air sermon, at Winchelsea, age 88.

October 8, 1781   Mrs. John Wesley dies at age 71. She is buried in Wandsworth.

Mary Vazeille, the widow whom John Wesley had married in 1751. She holds what appears to be a miniature portrait of John Wesley.

October 9, 1779   This night I lodged in the new house in London. How many more nights have I to spend here? —John Wesley's *Journal*

October

10

While I teach, I learn, says Seneca, and while I preach to others I instruct myself. And again, those are the best instructors, that teach by their lives and prove their words by their actions....While you instruct your children in the first principles of religion, be careful to impress a sense of them on your own mind, and ever take care of your affections, that they may keep pace with and be agreeable to your convictions of the great truths of natural and revealed religion.   —Susanna Wesley

11

October 11, 1709 from Susanna Wesley to her son "Sammy" several months after the great fire at Epworth:

Recovery from Misfortunes
Though nothing in the world could ever make me forget you, or prevent my having the tenderest regard for your happiness, and concern for your immortal soul; yet my mind has been so terribly shocked by our late misfortunes that though I cannot say I never had leisure, yet I could not dispose my self to write to you. A long series of adverse fortunes had before inclined me to a too melancholic tempest, but this most strange and not surprising accident attended by so many calamitous circumstances gave my soul so strong a bent to extreme sadness that I have not been able to recover myself till a few days; but have been as one dead to the world, incapable of enjoying any of those comforts which God in His mercy hath yet left me.

Interior of St. Andrew's church, Epworth, where the Wesley family attended church for 39 years.

The Vows of God are upon You

Now I am, Heaven be praised, a little free from that unhappy paroxysm, the first thing I shall inquire after is the health of your soul. I hope you retain the impressions of your education, nor have forgot that the vows of God are upon you. You know that the first fruits are His by an unalterable right, and that as your parents devoted you to the service of the Almighty, so you yourself made it your choice when your father was offered another way for your subsistence. But have you duly weighed what such a choice, and such a dedication imports? Sammy, consider what purity, what devotion! what separation from the world! what exemplary virtues are required in those who are to guide others in their way to Glory! Exemplary I say, for low and common degrees of piety are not sufficient for those of your sacred function. You must not think to live like the rest of the world, but your light in a more special manner must so shine among men that they may see your good works and thereby be led to glorify your Father which is in Heaven.

Live Like His Disciples

For my part I cannot see how any clergyman can reprove sinners, or exhort men to lead a good life, when they themselves indulge their own corrupt inclinations and by their practice contradict their doctrine. If the holy Jesus be in truth their Master, and they are really his ambassadors, surely it becomes them to live like his disciples, and if they do not, what a sad account they must one day give of their stewardship, you would do well to consider.

Wean Yourself

Nor would I have you now give yourself liberty to comply with the vain or sinful customs of the world, foolishly flattering yourself that it will be time enough to begin a strict course of life when you enter into orders, when the eyes of the world will be more upon you; for let me tell you Now is the time to lay a good foundation, now is the time to wean yourself from vanity, and sensual pleasures; if you indulge your unruly passions, if now you suffer yourself to love the world or anything in it more than God, if you now neglect your private duties, your daily sacrifices of prayers and thanksgiving, or grow remiss or cold in their performance; if now you permit impurity, anger, hatred, malice, or any kind of intemper-

October

Samuel Wesley, Jr., who was 19 years old and at school in London when his mother wrote this letter to him.

ance to gain an ascendant over your mind, you are in danger of being earnestly lost. Believe me, first motions are most easy to restrain, if they pass unheeded, and unchecked, how soon do they prevail upon the inclination and when that point is gained, how insensibly are we led into Act, which being multiplied, naturally beget a Habit; and how hard that is to be cured you very well know.

A Certain Method
First I would advise you as far as is possible in your present circumstances to throw all your business into a certain method, by which means you'll learn to improve every precious moment, and find an unspeakable facility in the performance of your respective duties. Begin and end the day with Him who is the Alpha and Omega, and though my ignorance of the orders of the school make it impossible for me to assign what time you should spend in private devotions, yet I'm sure if you do but really experience what it is to love God, you'll redeem all the time you can for His more immediate service. What is in your own power you may dispose of, nor are your rules so strict as not to admit of some diversions.

Time for Recreation

I'll tell you what method I used to observe when I was in my father's house, and perhaps had as little if not less liberty than you have now. I used to allow myself as much time for recreation as I spent in private devotion; not that I always spent so much, but so far I gave myself leave to go but no farther. So likewise in all things else, appoint so much time for sleep, eating, company....

Observance of the Lord's Day

But above all things, my dear Sammy, I command you, I beg, I beseech you to be very strict in your observance of the Lord's Day. That blessed day of God, that most dear and sacred type of the great Sabbath which we hope to enjoy with Him in Glory. Believe me, Dear Child, there is more depends on this one duty than the unthinking world is aware of. I am verily persuaded that our most gracious God is more ready to grant our petitions and more pleased with our devotions on that day than any other....

John and Charles Wesley embark at Gravesend to sail for Georgia. Asked what she felt about her sons setting off for such distant lands, Susanna replied, "Had I twenty sons, I should rejoice that they were all so employed, though I should never see them more."

12

October 12, 1726 Sarah Gwynne born (later Mrs. Charles Wesley)

October 12, 1781 I was informed my wife died on Monday. This evening she was buried, though I was not informed of it till a day or two after! —John Wesley's *Journal*

13

Six parts of time to thee are freely given;
The seventh is sacred, and reserved by Heaven.
If long thou wishest to enjoy thy land,
Obey thy parents in each just command.
    —Samuel Wesley, from the Ten Commandments
    as rephrased in *The Life of Christ*

Leviathan, a crocodile engraved for Samuel Wesley's 'Dissertations on the Book of Job.'

14

.October 14, 1735 Mr. Benjamin Ingham, of Queen's College, Oxford, Mr. Charles Delamotte, son of a merchant in London, my brother Charles Wesley, and myself, took boat for Gravesend, in order to embark for Georgia. Our end in leaving our native country was not to avoid want (God having given us plenty of temporal blessings), nor to gain the dung or dross of riches or honor; but simply this, to save our souls; to live wholly to the glory of God. In the afternoon we found the *Simmonds* off Gravesend, and immediately went on board. —John Wesley's *Journal*

October 15, 1730 A fit of the stone lasted me three **15**
weeks and ever since Dr. Greathead has been setting me
up again. I am now got very well again and laugh at
those things which disturbed me when I am sick. You I
believe to be my friend (note I take Friend in a much
stricter sense than most in the world do, namely for one
who partakes in all my fortunes, who mourns when any
trouble seizes me, who rejoices when any Good comes to
me, and thinks himself happy when in anything he can
contribute to my satisfaction.) —Emily Wesley to her
brother John

Every hour of every day you are laid upon my heart....I **16**
cannot doubt that our next will be our happiest meeting.
—Charles Wesley to his wife

Samuel, son of Charles and Sarah Wesley.

17

With regard to a real judge of music disliking Haydn and Mozart, it is a thing so strange to me that I have been frequently endeavoring how to account for it. Haydn and Mozart must be heard often before they are thoroughly understood, as it strikes me, even by those who have heard much music of more gradual modulation; but I do think that when the ear and mind become perfectly habituated to their rapid successions of harmony the feast is rich indeed, and the surprise is still maintained notwithstanding familiarity, which to me is a very extraordinary circumstance. —Samuel Wesley, Charles' son, to his brother Charles, 1807

18

Cleanse Thou me from secret faults, for out of the abundance of the heart the mouth speaketh. —Susanna Wesley *Meditations*

19

October 19, 1739 At four I preached at the Shire Hall of Cardiff again, where many gentry, I found, were present. Such freedom of speech I have seldom had, as was given me in explaining those words: "The kingdom of God is not meat and drink, but righteousness, and peace, and joy in the Holy Ghost." At six almost the whole town (I was informed) came together; to whom I explained the six last beatitudes: but my heart was so enlarged, I knew not how to give over, so that we continued three hours. —John Wesley's *Journal*

20

October 20, 1787 I have often repented of judging too severely, but very seldom of being too merciful. —John Wesley, Letter to Robert Carr Brackenbury

October 21, 1735   We sailed from Gravesend. Our common way of living was this: From four in the morning till five, each of us used private prayer. From five to seven we read the Bible together, carefully comparing it with the writings of the earliest ages. At seven we breakfasted. At eight were the public prayers. From nine to twelve I usually learned German, and Mr. Delamotte, Greek. My brother writ sermons, and Mr. Ingham instructed the children.

At twelve we met to give an account to one another what we had done since our last meeting, and what we designed to do before our next. About one we dined. The time from dinner to four, we spent in reading to those whom each of us had taken in charge, or in speaking to them severally, as need required. At four were the evening prayers; when either the second lesson was explained (as it always was in the morning), or the children were catechised and instructed before the congregation. From five to six we again used private prayer.

From six to seven I read in our cabin to two or three of the passsengers (of whom there were about eighty English on board), and each of my brethren to a few more in theirs. At seven I joined with the Germans in their public service; while Mr. Ingham was reading between the decks to as many as desired to hear. At eight we met again to exhort and instruct one another. Between nine and ten we went to bed, where neither the roaring of the sea, nor the motion of the ship, could take away the refreshing sleep which God gave us.

[The trip took 16 weeks; they anchored in the Savannah River on February 5, 1736.]

In the first place, pray take notice this is address'd only to those that buy the book, for such as only borrow it, my good friend the Bookseller and I will have nothing to do with them.   —Samuel Wesley, Preface to *Maggots,* a book of poems that was his first published work.

October

23

Frontispiece to Maggots, *Samuel Wesley's earliest book of poems, featuring a portrait of the author.*

24

October 24, 1769   This evening there was such an Aurora Borealis as I never saw before: the colors, both the white, the flame-color, and the scarlet, were so exceeding strong and beautiful. But they were awful, too: so that abundance of people were frighted into many good resolutions.   —John Wesley's *Journal*

25

October 25, 1789   Nothing will be too hard for you if you lean upon His strength and go on hand in hand, desiring only to do and suffer His holy and acceptable will. —John Wesley to John Grace in Londonderry

I shall endeavor to be as resigned and cheerful as possible to whatever God is pleased to ordain for me. He could as easily have blessed me with indulgent parents as others...if He had seen I could have born it. 'Tis certain an inferior cannot comprehend a superior wisdom.   —Kezzy Wesley to her brother John

A Tobacco Pipe

In the raw mornings when I'm freezing ripe
What compare with a tobacco pipe?...
I have a universal medicine chose
Which warms at once my guts, and hands, and nose....
When such as use my pipe but wisely will
Employ its aid to cure and not to kill;
Not Bezoar stone, nor that miraculous Horn
Which decks the strange invisible Unicorn
Can deadly poisons subtle streams, as well
As my tobacco pipe, when charged, dispel.
With this was Herchord acquainted; when
He smoked, and writ, and spit and smoked again.
Poets the glass with fancy do inspire,
The pipe mounts our philosopher far higher;
And molds him syllogisms tough and strong
And polishes his labors all along.
Sure when Prometheus climbed above the poles
Slyly to learn their art of making souls,
When of his fire he fretting Jove did swipe,
He stole it thence in a tobacco pipe.*
    —Samuel Wesley, *Maggots*

October 28, 1765   I breakfasted with Mr. Whitefield, who seemed to be an old, old man, being fairly worn out in his Master's service, though he has hardly seen fifty years; and yet it pleases God that I, who am now in my sixty-third year, find no disorder, no weakness, no decay, no difference from what I was at five-and-twenty; only that I have fewer teeth and more grey hairs.
—John Wesley's *Journal*

October

29

Help me, O Lord, to make a true use of all disappointments and calamities in this life, in such a way that they may unite my heart more closely with Thee.   —Susanna Wesley, *Meditations*

30

Jesus, the first and last,
On Thee my soul is cast;
Thou didst Thy work begin
By blotting out my sin;
Thou wilt the root remove,
And perfect me in love.

Yet when the work is done,
The work is but begun;
Partaker of Thy grace,
I long to see Thy face;
The first I prove below,
The last I die to know.
     —Charles Wesley

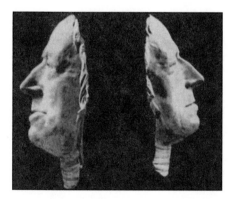

This death mask was cast from John Wesley's face within three or four hours of his death.

NOVEMBER

The New Chapel in City Road, London, opened November 1, 1778

November 1, 1734 Mary Wesley Whitelamb dies at Wroote after childbirth, age 38.

Epitaph, written by her sister Hetty

> If highest worth, in beauty's bloom,
> Exempted mortals from the Tomb,
> We had not round this sacred Bier
> Mourned the sweet Babe and Mother here,
> Where innocence from harm is blest,
> And the meek sufferer is at rest!
> Fierce pangs she bore without complaint,
> Till heaven relieved the finish'd Saint.
>   If savage bosoms felt her woe
> (Who lived and died without a foe)
> How should I mourn, or how commend,
> My tenderest, dearest, *firmest* friend?
> Most pious, meek, resign'd, and chaste,
> With every social virtue graced!
>   If, Reader, thou wouldst prove, and know,
> The ease she found not here below;
> Her bright example points the way
> To perfect bliss and endless day.

November

2

[November 1, 1778] was the day appointed for opening the new chapel in the City Road. It is perfectly neat, but not fine; and contains far more people than the Foundery. Many were afraid that the multitudes, crowding from all parts, would have occasioned much disturbance. But they were happily disappointed: there was none at all: all was quietness, decency, and order. I preached on part of Solomon's Prayer at the Dedication of the Temple.
—John Wesley's *Journal*

3

November 3, 1742   Two of those who are called *prophets* desired to speak with me. They told me they were sent from God with a message to me; which was, that very shortly I should be born'd again. One of them added, they would stay in the house till it was done, unless I turned them out. I answered, gravely, "I will not turn you out," and showed them down into the society room. It was tolerably cold; and they had neither meat nor drink: however, there they sat from morning to evening. They then went quietly away, and I have heard nothing from them since.   —John Wesley's *Journal*

4

First let me ask you what you are in matters of Religion, and the power of godliness? For present forget your greatness, and give account of your goodness (if you have it).   —Dr. Samuel Annesley, addressing Parliament

5

November 5, 1756   Charles Wesley's published *Journal* ends.

Plaque on the house in Marylebone where Charles Wesley and his family lived, on what was then Chesterfield Street and is now Wheatley Street.

November 6, 1739   Samuel Wesley, Jr., dies after an illness of four hours. His memorial reads:

Here lye interred
The remains of the
Rev. Mr. SAMUEL WESLEY, A.M.,
Sometime student of Christ Church Oxon:
A man, for his uncommon wit and learning,
For the benevolence of his temper,
And simplicity of manners,
Deservedly beloved and esteemed by all:
An excellent preacher:
But whose best sermon
Was the constant example of an edifying life.
So continually and zealously employed
In acts of beneficence and charity,
That he truly followed
His blessed Master's example
In going about doing good:
Of such scrupulous integrity,
that he declined occasions of advancement in the
world,
Through fear of being involved in dangerous compli-
ances;
And avoided the usual ways of preferment
As studiously as many others seek them.
Therefore, after a life spent
In the laborious employment of teaching youth,
First for near twenty years
As one of the ushers in Westminster School,
Afterwards for seven years
As head master of the free School at Tiverton,
He resigned his soul to God
November 6th, 1739, in the 49th year of his age.

November 7, 1739   At eight our society met at Fetter Lane. We sat an hour without speaking. The rest of the time was spent in dispute.   —John Wesley's *Journal*

November

8

At nine I passed through Thorpe. I asked my companion, "Where are the pretty wild creatures that were for braining me and my horse, the last time I came this way?" He told me they had lost their spirit with their Captain, a woman, the bitterest of them all, who died lately in horrible despair. This quite terrified our enemies. Her daughter is now a believer, and several others in the place: nay, they have even got a Society among them.   —Charles Wesley's *Journal*

9

I read prayers, and Mr. Whitefield preached. How wise is God in giving different talents to different preachers! Even the little improprieties both of his language and manner were a means of profiting many, who would not have been touched by a more correct discourse, or a more calm and regular manner of speaking.   —John Wesley's *Journal*

The Chapel in Fetter Lane

10

Hear Him, ye deaf; His praise, ye dumb,
Your loosen'd tongues employ;
Ye blind, behold your Savior come;
And leap, ye lame, for joy!
from **O for a thousand tongues to sing**
  —Charles Wesley

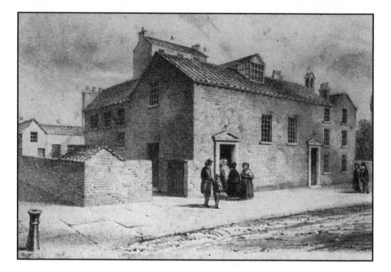

The Foundery, center of the Methodist movement in London until City Road Chapel opened in 1778. John Wesley lived here. Susanna Wesley spent her last years and died here.

November 11, 1739   John Wesley preaches his first sermon at the Foundery.

11

November 12, 1688   Samuel and Susanna Wesley marry, in London.

12

Samuel and Susanna Wesley. Drawing by Richard Douglas.

November

13

[John, outlining the desirability of Grace Murray, whom he planned to marry. The union was prevented by Charles' interference. She married John Bennet, a Methodist preacher, and for years was a tireless worker in the Methodist movement.]

First, as a housekeeper she has every qualification I desire.
She is remarkably neat in person, in clothes, in all things.
She is nicely frugal, yet not sordid.
As a nurse (which my poor shattered, enfeebled carcass now frequently stands in need of) she is careful to the last degree, indefatigably patient and inexpressibly tender... She understands my constitution better than most physicians.
As a companion she has good sense and some knowledge both of men and books. She is of engaging temper and of a mild, sprightly, cheerful and yet serious nature.
As a friend she has been long tried and found faithful.
Lastly, as a fellow laborer in the Gospel of Christ (the light wherein my wife is to be chiefly considered) she has in a measure which I never found in any other both grace and gifts and fruit.
She is and would be a continual defence (under God) against unholy desires and inordinate affections which I never did entirely conquer for six months together. She would likewise remove many hindrances from others, women in particular. She would guard many from inordinate affection for me, to which they would be far less exposed.   —John Wesley

14

November 14, 1661 Dr. Samuel Annesley signs his editorial preface to *The Morning Exercise at Cripplegate: or, Several Cases of Conscience Practically Resolved, by Sundry Ministers, September 1661.*

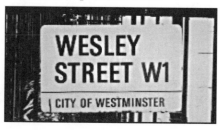

A Marylebone street near Charles Wesley's house is named after its famous neighbors.

Sarah Wesley ("junior") sent her brother Charles what she called "a lively representation" of the scene outside church one evening after her father preached. She includes this key:

No 1   The Revd Mr. CW coming from square Preaching. The painter had not time to take a stronger likeness
No 2   Brother Tenant; who is going to introduce him to a sett of colliers
No 3   The first collier; who holds out his Hand and stands on one leg for you
No 4   This collier politely waits till his neighbour has shaken hands
No 5   The Revd CW daughter; she has a sweet smile upon her face and stands patiently whilst her Papa shakes hands with *all* the colliers, not knowing but she must do so too. A perfect pattern! Dear Lady!

November

No 6   A Methodist sister; lamenting the vanity of dress in Miss W

No 7   Another, who agrees in the lamentation most outrageously

No 8   A *Kingswood Friend* who is sliding in the crowd

No 9   Mr May the shoemaker; who has many advantages; he can look over the peoples heads, and has a fine *oblique view* of the Revd CW family

No 10   A collier who tells his companion what they wait for

No 11   His companion rejoices in the hope of squeezing Mr. CW's hand

No 12   The crowd of colliers marching forward also

No 13   A Brother in notwithstanding [sic] a woman of *deep experience*

16

17

The touch of the organ [at Westminster Abbey] is remarkably good, indeed rather too light for me. It is a complete contrast with St. Paul's, where you may remember that the keys are all as stubborn as Fox's Martyrs, and bear almost as much buffeting. — Samuel Wesley, Jr., Charles' son, to his brother Charles, 1807

18

November 18, 1682   Dr. Samuel Annesley's house "broke into" by informers, to seize goods to pay for fines levied against him for conducting Nonconformist worship services. His daughter Susanna is 13 years old at the time.

19

Let none think his labor of love is lost because the fruit does not immediately appear! Near forty years did my father labor here; but he saw little fruit of all his labor. I took some pains among this people too, and my strength also seemed spent in vain; but now the fruit appeared. —John Wesley's *Journal,* writing of Epworth

20

November 20, 1785   At three in the morning two or three men broke into our house, through the kitchen window. Thence they came up into the parlor, and broke open Mr. Moore's bureau, where they found two or three pounds: the night before I had prevented his leaving there seventy pounds, which he had just received. They next broke open the cupboard, and took away some silver spoons. Just at this time the alarm, which Mr. Moore by mistake had set for half-past three (instead of four), went off, as it usually did, with a thundering noise. At this the thieves ran away with all speed though their work was not half done; and the whole damage which we sustained scarce amounted to six pounds. —John Wesley's *Journal*

Opposite page: St. Andrew's Church, Epworth

November

21

In the esteem of the world, they pass for kind and indulgent, whom I call cruel parents; who permit their children to get habits which they know must be afterwards broken. Nay, some are so stupidly fond as in sport to teach their children to do things which in a while after they have severely beaten them for doing. —Susanna Wesley

22

This then is the salvation which is through faith, even in the present world: a salvation from sin and the consequences of sin, both often expressed in the word 'justification,' which, taken in the largest sense, implies a deliverance from guilt and punishment, by the atonement of Christ actually applied to the soul of the sinner now believing on him, and a deliverance from the power of sin, through Christ 'formed in his heart,' so that he who is thus justified or saved by faith is indeed 'born again.' —John Wesley, Sermon 1, *Salvation by Faith* (1738)

23

I believe three things must go together in our justification: upon God's part, His great mercy and grace; upon Christ's part, the satisfaction of God's justice, by the offering His body and shedding His blood, 'and fulfilling the law of God perfectly'; and upon our part, true and living faith in the merits of Jesus Christ. —John Wesley, *The Principles of a Methodist* (1742)

November

24

By 'perfection' I mean 'perfect love,' or the loving God with all our heart, so as to rejoice evermore, to pray without ceasing, and in everything to give thanks. I am convinced every believer may attain this; yet I do not say he is in a state of damnation or under the curse of God till he does attain. No, he is in a state of grace and in favor with God as long as he believes.   —John Wesley, Letter to Elizabeth Hardy

25

Be thou a guide to them that travel by land or water. Give a strong and quiet spirit to those who are condemned to death, liberty to prisoners and captives, and ease and cheerfulness to every sad heart.   —John Wesley, a prayer

26

I will freely own that, strictly speaking, I never did want bread. But then, I had so much care to get it before it was eat, and to pay for it after, as has often made it very unpleasant to me. And I think to have bread on such terms is the next degree of wretchedness to having none at all.   —Susanna Wesley

27

A block from a quilt of "linsey-woolsey" spun and woven in the Epworth Rectory some-time between 1710-1735. Only this frag-ment remains.

November

28

A Minister's whole being should be in his Ministry; his soul, his body, his time, all his graces, all his learning, all his studies, all his interests, all laid out in the work of *the* Ministry. —Dr. Samuel Annesley

29

I design plain truth for plain people. Therefore of set purpose I abstain from all nice and philosophical speculations, from all perplexed and intricate reasonings, and as far as possible from even the show of learning, unless in sometimes citing the original Scriptures. I labor to avoid all words which are not easy to be understood, all which are not used in common life....Yet I am not assured that I do not slide into them unawares; it is so extremely natural to imagine that a word which is familiar to ourselves is so to all the world. —John Wesley, Preface to *Sermons on Several Occasions* (1746)

30

Lo, he comes with clouds descending,
Once for favored sinners slain;
Thousand, thousand saints attending
Swell the triumph of his train.
Hallelujah! Hallelujah!
God appears on earth to reign.

Yea, Amen! Let all adore Thee,
High on Thy eternal throne;
Savior, take the power and glory,
Claim the kingdom for thine own.
Hallelujah! Hallelujah!
Everlasting God, come down!*
  —Charles Wesley

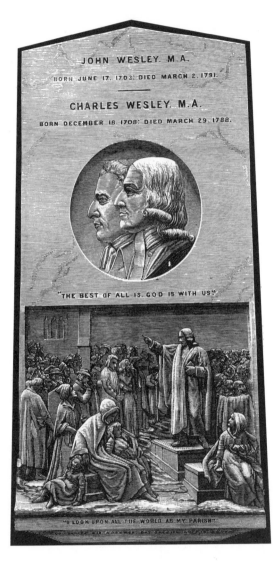

The memorial to John and Charles Wesley in Westminster Abbey.

1

December 1, 1781   I am never so busy as to forget my friends.   —John Wesley, Letter to Mrs. Downes

2

December 2, 1725   Anne Wesley marries John Lambert in Finningly. Her brother Samuel writes a poem that concludes:

> The greatest earthly pleasure try,
> Allowed by Providence Divine;
> Be he a husband blest as I.
> And thou a wife as good as mine!*

3

Those that are without or reject the Sunshine of Scripture, yet they cannot blow out God's Candle of Conscience.   —Dr. Samuel Annesley

4

Nay, to high heaven for greater gifts I bend;
Health I've enjoyed, and I had once a friend!
    —Hetty Wesley

5

O Thou who camest from above,
The pure celestial fire to impart,
Kindle a flame of sacred love
On the mean altar of my heart.

There let it for Thy glory burn
With inextinguishable blaze,
And trembling to its source return
In humble prayer, and fervent praise.*
    —Charles Wesley

6

I thank Thee, O God, because I know that religion does not mean melancholy and moroseness.....When I am peevish and morose, it is not because of religion, but of my want of it.   —Susanna Wesley

December

December 7, 1764 Susanna Wesley Ellison dies in London, age 69.

Sister Sukey was in huge agonies for five days, and then died in full assurance of faith. Some of her last words (after she had been speechless for some time) were, "Jesus is come! Heaven is here!" —John Wesley, Letter to Charles

December 8, 1742 [In Newcastle, the society buys ground to build the Orphan House — which in fact is never used to house orphans, but for preaching, meeting, and study:] Mr. Stephenson and I signed an article, and I took possession of the ground....The whole is about forty yards in length; in the middle of which we determined to build the house, leaving room for a small courtyard before, and a little garden behind, the building.
—John Wesley's *Journal*

"The lower part of the 'House' was the chapel, fitted up with pulpit and forms; the men and women sitting apart. Galleries were subsequently erected....Above the chapel was a large compartment lighted from behind, the center of which was used as a band-room; opening from which, on either side, were several classrooms for the use of the Society. On the highest story —a kind of Scotch 'flat'— were suites of apartments, subsequently appropriated for the residence of the preachers and their families; while on the roof was a wooden erection about eleven feet square with tiled covering, generally known as 'Mr. Wesley's study.' This apartment, even in the tidiest days of the Orphan House, must have been of the most homely description. The fireplace would, in this day, be repudiated by the most humble cottager. In strict keeping with it were the door and furniture of the room. Its exposure to the wintry blasts of the north would also render it an undesirable retreat for any to whom warmth and comfort were matters of moment. Such, however, was the apartment designed and appropriated by the self-denying Wesley for his special residence when sojourning in Newcastle. Here, at different periods, much of his valuable time was spent: here also, as various intimations in his Journal show, he loved to be." [W.W.Stamp, 1863]

9

What shall I do my God to love,
My loving God to praise?
The length, and breadth, and height to prove
And depth of sovereign grace?

Come quickly, gracious Lord, and take
Possession of Thine own;
My longing heart vouchsafe to make
Thine everlasting throne.
　　—Charles Wesley

10

Our heart danced for joy, and in our song did we praise Him.　—Charles Wesley's *Journal*

11

It is one thing to have faith, and another thing to be sensible we have it.　—Susanna to Charles

---

December

I removed into a lodging adjoining to the ground where we were preparing to build [the orphan House in Newcastle]; but the violent frost obliged us to delay the work. I never felt so intense cold before. In a room where a constant fire was kept, though my desk was fixed within a yard of the chimney, I could not write for a quarter of an hour together without my hands being quite benumbed.   —John Wesley's *Journal*

Below: John Wesley's electric machine, used in his clinic. Among health problems he believed electrifying in a proper manner could cure he listed coldness of the feet, deafness, gout, palpitations, sciatica, shingles, and toothache.

In consequence of reading Dr. Cheyne, I chose to eat sparingly, and drink water. This was another great means of continuing my health.   —John Wesley's *Journal*

December

15

Let the preaching at five in the morning be constantly kept up, whenever you can have twenty hearers. This is the glory of the Methodists! Whenever this is dropped, they will dwindle away into nothing. Rising early is equally good for soul and body. It helps the nerves better than a thousand medicines; and, in particular, preserves the sight, and prevents lowness of spirits, more than can be well imagined. —John Wesley at the Bristol Conference of 1768

16

I mentioned to the society my design of giving physic to the poor. About thirty came the next day, and in three weeks about three hundred. This we continued for several years, till the number of patients still increasing, the expense was greater than we could bear: meantime, through the blessing of God, many who had been ill for months or years were restored to perfect health. —John Wesley's *Journal*

17

The Rev. John Westley, father of Samuel Wesley. He died while his son was just a child.

December 17, 1662 Samuel Wesley, Sr., son of Rev. and Mrs. John Westley, baptised at Winterborn-Whitchurch, Dorset.

December 18, 1707 Charles Wesley born, 18th child of Samuel and Susanna Wesley, in Epworth. This date, like many birthdates for the Wesleys, is conjectural. His baptismal date is December 29, 1707. Charles arrived several weeks before he was due, so they kept him wrapped in wool until the date he should have been born. Tradition says he neither cried nor opened his eyes until then. Arguably the first Methodist — it was he who first formed the Holy Club at Oxford that earned the nickname "Methodists" — he was an extremely persuasive and popular preacher. He is now remembered chiefly for having written the verses of over 6000 hymns and is called "the sweet singer of Methodism."

But still strait is the gate and narrow is the way that leadeth unto life and what is yet worse, few, comparatively very few there be that find it. This thought often damps my devotion and retards the soul when it should aspire towards heaven. How know I whether or not I shall persevere? How shall I be assured that the world, the flesh, the Devil shall never be too hard for me? It is true I know that all things in this world are vain, perishing, unsatisfactory enjoyments, that all is vanity and vexation of spirit; but still I do not find that the mind has such a strong sense of these things, but that unforseen accidents, hopes, company often strongly allure it to a liking and compliance for sensual delights, and I am often apt to say, It is good to be here. —Susanna Wesley

Reason alone cannot produce hope in any child of man....This hope can only spring from Christian faith: therefore where there is not faith, there is not hope. —John Wesley, Sermon 70, *The Case of Reason Impartially Considered* (1781)

December 21, 1733 Mary Wesley marries John Whitelamb. He had served as her father's assistant and amaneunsis. The Wesley's had helped to send the young man to Oxford and Samuel was responsible for gaining him the assignment to Wroote, which had formerly been part of Samuel's cure. Mary and John live very happily at Wroote for just one year before she dies. He remains rector there for 35 years until his death.

December 22, 1822 Sarah Gwynne Wesley, Charles's wife, dies, age 96.

December 22, 1787 I yielded to the importunity of a painter and sat an hour and a half in all for my portrait. I think it was the best that ever was taken. —John Wesley's *Journal*

Below: the portrait referred to, painted by William Hamilton, R.A.

December 23, 1736   Mr. Delamotte and I, with a guide, set out to walk to the Cowpen. When we had walked two or three hours, our guide told us plainly, he did not know where we were. However, believing it could not be far off, we thought it best to go on. In an hour or two we came to a cypress swamp, which lay directly across our way: there was not time to walk back to Savannah before night; so we walked through it, the water being about breast high.

By the time we had gone a mile beyond it, we were out of all path; and it being now past sunset, we sat down, intending to make a fire, and to stay there till morning; but finding our tinder wet, we were at a stand. I advised to walk on still; but my companions, being faint and weary, were for lying down, which we accordingly did about six o'clock: the ground was as wet as our clothes, which, it being a sharp frost, were soon froze together; however, I slept till six in the morning.

There fell a heavy dew in the night, which covered us over as white as snow. Within an hour after sunrise, we came to a plantation; and in the evening, without any hurt, to Savannah. [On the 28th, he records "We set out by land with a better guide."]   —John Wesley's *Journal*

Statue of Charles Wesley outside the New Room in Bristol.

24

Come, thou long-expected Jesus
Born to set Thy People free,
From our fears and sins release us,
Let us find our rest in Thee.

Israel's strength and consolation,
Hope of all the earth Thou art;
Dear Desire of every nation,
Joy of every longing heart.

Born Thy people to deliver,
Born a child and yet a king,
Born to reign in us for ever,
Now Thy gracious Kingdom bring.

By Thine own eternal Spirit
Rule in all our hearts alone;
By Thine all-sufficient merit
Raise us to Thy glorious throne.
　　—Charles Wesley

25

Love Divine, all loves excelling,
Joy of heaven, to earth come down;
Fix in us Thy humble dwelling,
All Thy faithful mercies crown:
Jesu, Thou art all compassion,
Pure, unbounded love Thou art;
Visit us with Thy salvation,
Enter every trembling heart.*
　　—Charles Wesley

26

The best of all is, God is with us.
—Spoken by John Wesley on his deathbed.

December

December 27, 1726   Hetty Wesley's first child, a girl, buried at Louth, age 10 months. All her children die at birth or in infancy.

A Mother's Address to Her Dying Infant

Tender softness, infant mild,
Perfect, purest, brightest Child!
Transient lustre, beauteous clay,
Smiling wonder of a day!
Ere the last convulsive start
Rend thy unresisting heart,
Ere the long-enduring swoon
Weigh thy precious eyelids down,
Ah, regard a mother's moan!
Anguish deeper than thy own.*
     —Mehetabel "Hetty" Wesley Wright

December 28, 1740   Among my visitants this morning I had a very ingenious person, who generously proffered to teach me the grand arcanum [secret of alchemy] for the value of five shillings. Having no need of money, I declined his proffer; but gave him sixpence, and told him, as he had the art of transmutation, it was the same as if I had given him half a guinea.   —Charles Wesley's *Journal*

Hark! the herald angels sing,
"Glory to the newborn King;
Peace on earth, and mercy mild,
God and sinners reconciled!"
Joyful, all ye nations, rise,
Join the triumph of the skies;
With th'angelic host proclaim,
"Christ is born in Bethlehem!"
Hark! the herald angels sing,
"Glory to the newborn King!"*
     —Charles Wesley

December

30

December 30, 1771   At my brother's request, I sat again for my picture. This melancholy employment always reminds me of that natural reflection,

> "Behold what frailty we in man may see!
> His shadow is less given to change than he."
> —John Wesley's *Journal*

31

December 31, 1696   Dr. Samuel Annesley, Susanna Annesley Wesley's father, dies in London, age 77. He bequeathes to Susanna his valuable papers and manuscripts, which tragically burn in the rectory fire of 1709. Normally of a very strong constitution, he has suffered an extremely painful disorder which, after 17 weeks, terminates in his death. Just before his departure it is reported that his joy is so great that in an ecstasy he cries out, "I cannot contain it! What manner of love is this to a poor worm? I cannot express a thousandth part of what praise is due to Thee. It is but little I can give Thee; but, Lord, help me to give Thee my all, and rejoice that others can praise Thee better. I shall be satisfied with Thy likeness. Satisfied! Satisfied! O my dear Jesus, I come."

The home of the Wesley family, the Old Rectory at Epworth

December

Bibliography and Further Reading

Baker, Frank, ed. *The Works of John Wesley*. Oxford: Clarendon Press, 1980.

Brailsford, Mabel Richmond. *A Tale of Two Brothers*. NY: Oxford University Press, 1954.

Clarke, Adam. *Memoirs of the Wesley Family*. NY: N. Bangs and T. Mason, for The Methodist Episcopal Church, 1824.

Curnock, Nehemiah. *John Wesley's Journal, Abridged*. London: The Epworth Press, reprint 1967.

Doughty, W. L. *The Prayers of Susanna Wesley*. Grand Rapids: Zondervan Publishing House, 1984.

Dove, John. *The Wesley Family*. London: Simpkin & Marshall, 1833.

Edwards, W. Le Cato. *Epworth...the Home of the Wesleys*. ND.

Edwards, Maldwyn. *My Dear Sister*. Manchester: Penwork (Leeds) Ltd., N.D.

Gill, Frederick C. *Charles Wesley, The First Methodist*. Nashville and NY: Abingdon Press, 1964.

Greetham, Mary and Peter. *Samuel Wesley*. Peterborough: Foundery Press, 1990.

Harmon, Rebecca Lamar. *Susanna, Mother of the Wesleys*. Nashville and NY: Abingdon Press, 1968.

Jackson, Thomas. *The Life of the Rev. Charles Wesley, M.A., Sometime Student of Christ Church, Oxford*. NY: G. Lane & P. P. Sanford, 1844.

——*The Journal of the Rev. Charles Wesley*. London: John Mason, 1849.

Jarboe, Betty M. *Wesley Quotations*. Metuchen, NJ, & London: The Scarecrow Press, Inc., 1990.

Kirk, John. *The Mother of the Wesleys: A Biography*. Cincinnati, 1865.

Lee, Umphrey. *The Lord's Horseman*. Nashville and NY: Abingdon Press, 1954.

Longworth, Allan. *Samuel Wesley Junior*. Peterborough: Foundery Press, 1991.

Maser, Frederick E. *Seven Sisters in Search of Love*. Rutland, VT: Academy Books, 1988.

Methodist History, a quarterly published by the General Commission on Archives and History of the United Methodist Church, Madison, NJ.

Milburn, Geoffrey E. *The Travelling Preacher: John Wesley in the North East 1742-1790*. Wesley Historical Society (North East Branch), 1987.

Newton, John A. *Susanna Wesley and the Puritan Tradition in Methodism*. London: Epworth Press, 1968.

Pearce, John. *The Wesleys in Cornwall*. Truro: D. Bradford Barton Ltd., 1964.

Pellowe, Wm. C. S. *John Wesley, Master in Religion*. Methodist Episcopal Church South, 1933.

Quiller-Couch, Sir Arthur. *Hetty Wesley*. London: The Amalgamated Press, Ltd., N.D.

Southey, Robert. *The Life of Wesley*. London: Frederick Warne and Co., 1893.

W. W. Stamp. *The Orphan House of Wesley with Notices of Early Methodism in Newcastle upon Tyne and its Vicinity*, 1863.

Stevenson, George John. *Memorials of the Wesley Family*. London: S. W. Partridge & Co., 1876.

Telford, John, ed. *The Letters of the Rev. John Wesley, A.M., Sometime Fellow of Lincoln College, Oxford*. London: The Epworth Press, 1931.

Telford, John, ed. *Sayings and Portraits of Charles Wesley*. London: The Epworth Press, 1927.

Telford, John, ed. *Sayings and Portraits of John Wesley*. London: The Epworth Press, 1924.

Tyerman, Luke. *The Life and Times of the Rev. John Wesley, M.A.* NY: Harper, 1872.

Wesley, Charles. *Hymns Occasioned by the Earthquake*. Bristol: 1756.

Wesley, John. *Primitive Physic*. William H. Paynter, ed. Plymouth: Parade Printing Works Ltd., 1961.

Wesley, Samuel, A.M., Jun. *Poems on Several Occasions*. London: Simpkin, Marshall, & Co., 1862.

Wesley, Samuel. *Maggots*. London: Printed for John Dunton at the Sign of the Black Raven, at the Corner of Princes Street near the Royal Exchange, 1685.

——*Dissertationes in Librum Jobi*. 1736.

——*The Life of our Blessed Lord and Saviour Jesus Christ*. London, 1697.

——*A defense of a letter concerning the education of Dissenters in their private academies*. 1704.

Wesley Family Papers. Methodist Archives and Research Centre, John Rylands University Library of Manchester.

Wesley His Own Biographer. London: C. H. Kelly, 1891.

Wright, David and Jill. *30 Hymns of the Wesleys*. Exeter: Paternoster Press, 1985.

CREDITS FOR ILLUSTRATIONS

January

1 Epworth Rectory, old engraving from Adam Clarke, *Memoirs of the Wesley Family*. **4, 7** St. Andrew's Parish Church, Susanna Wesley: old engravings: Courtesy of Richard Douglas. **12** Kingswood School: *Wesley His Own Biographer*. **14, 17** Behemoth, Samuel Wesley: *Dissertations on the Book of Job*. **20** Plaque and Susanna Annesley Wesley's birthplace: photos by Mark Trewin. **22** John Wesley, engraving based on Williams' portrait: Permission and photograph: Wesley's Chapel, London. **24** Signatures: Adam Clarke's *Memoirs of the Wesley Family*. **28** Charterhouse engraving: *Wesley His Own Biographer*.

February

1 John Wesley by George Vertue: Copyright British Museum. **6** Samuel Annesley, LLD: Dr. Williams's Library, London. **9** Samuel Wesley engraving: Courtesy of Richard Douglas; Bedroom,kitchen at Epworth Old Rectory: Courtesy of Trustees of The Old Rectory; Fire engraving: *Wesley His Own Biographer;* Fire engraving: Courtesy of Richard Douglas. **10** Sammy and Susanna with cat: drawing by Richard Douglas. **19** Mary Vazeille (Mrs. John Wesley): Permission and photo courtesy of Methodist Church Overseas Division (Methodist Missionary Society), London. **21** Epworth market cross: photo by Susan Pellowe. **24** John Wesley engraving by Ridley: Wesley's Chapel, London.

March

1 *The Holy Triumph of John Wesley in His Dying* by Marshall Claxton, R.A.: Permission and photo courtesy of Methodist Church Overseas Division (Methodist Missionary Society), London. **13** Wroote Rectory: The Wesley Historical Society Library, Oxford, England. **17** Map of Holy Land: *Dissertations on the Book of Job*. **19** Pensford bull: *Wesley His Own Biographer*. **24** *Susanna Wesley* by Forster: Wesley's Chapel, London. **27** Wesley's Tomb and City Road Chapel Reflected in Buildings: photo by A.F. Kersting. **28** John Wesley statue at City Road Chapel: photo by Susan Pellowe.

April

1 Westminster School, London: *Wesley His Own Biographer.* **5** Charles Wesley monument at St. Marylebone parish church: photo by Mark Trewin. **8** Charles and Sarah Wesley's home at No. 4 Charles Street in Bristol: Courtesy of John Wesley's Chapel, The New Room, Bristol; photo by Mark R. Wallis; *Sarah Gwynne* by John Russell, R.A.: Courtesy of John Wesley's Chapel, The New Room, Bristol; photo by Mark R. Wallis. **13** Dr. Samuel Annesley: Dr. Williams's Library, London. **20** John Wesley on Horseback: Courtesy of John Wesley's Chapel, The New Room, Bristol; photo by Mark R. Wallis. **24** John Wesley with Dr. Hamilton and Rev. Cole in Edinburgh: Wesley's Chapel, London. **25** Rev. Samuel Wesley's tombstone: The Wesley Historical Society Library, Oxford, England. *30 Reverend John Wesley* by George Romney: Philadelphia Museum of Art: The John H. McFadden Collection.

May

1 *Charles Wesley* by John Russell, R.A.: Permission and photo courtesy of Methodist Church Overseas Division (Methodist Missionary Society), London. **4** John Wesley engraving by T.A.Dean: Wesley's Chapel, London. **9** *Mrs. Sarah Wesley* attributed to John Russell, R.A.: With the permission of the Archives and History Committee of the Methodist Church (G.B.); photo: Peter Forsaith/Mark Bickerstaff. **10** *Samuel Wesley*, son of Charles and Sarah, by John Jackson: Wesley's Chapel, London; photo: Peter Forsaith/ Mark Bickerstaff. **12** The New Room at Bristol: Courtesy of John Wesley's Chapel, The New Room, Bristol; photo by Mark R. Wallis. **15** Charles Wesley, private collection. **21** Charles Wesley, stained glass at City Road Chapel: photo by Susan Pellowe. **23** Aldersgate monument, London: photo by Mark Trewin. **25** Foundery Organ at City Road Chapel: photo by Susan Pellowe. **28** The Old Rectory, Epworth: Courtesy of Trustees of The Old Rectory. **29** Horse and rider in undrained fenlands: Cambridge Central Library, Libraries and Heritage, Cambridgeshire County Council. **30** Charles Wesley engraving by Jonathan Spilsbury: By courtesy of the National Portrait Gallery, London.

June

1 *Charterhouse Portrait* of John Wesley, artist unknown: permission and photo from Old John Street United Methodist Church, New York City. **4** John Wesley preaching, stained glass: photo by Susan Pellowe. **5** Beau Nash print: *Wesley His Own Biographer.* **6** John Wesley Preaching on His Father's Tomb: Courtesy of Richard Douglas. **9** *John Wesley Preaching in the Open Air at Willybank* by Maria Spilsbury-Taylor: Wesley's Chapel, London. **17** Baptismal font at St. Andrew's parish church, Epworth: The Wesley Historical Society Library, Oxford, England. **23** Susanna Wesley: Courtesy of Trustees of The Old Rectory. **28** Detail of John Wesley on Horseback: Courtesy of John Wesley's Chapel, The New Room, Bristol; photo by Mark R. Wallis. **30** John Wesley's lantern: Wesley's Chapel, London; Kingwood School engraving by James Heath 1730, hand-colored: with permission of The Wesley Centre, Kingswood School Bath.

July

1 Charles and John Wesley on marble memorial in Westminster Abbey: photo by A.F. Kersting. **8** Susanna Wesley/believed to be Lady Rudd by T.A.Dean: Wesley's Chapel, London. **15** John Wesley's spurs: Wesley's Chapel, London. **22** Susanna Wesley's monument inscription at City Road: photo by Mark Trewin. **31** Charles Wesley attributed to Henry Hudson: Courtesy of Trustees of The Old Rectory.

August

1 Susanna Wesley's gravestone: photo by Susan Pellowe. **2, 5** Susanna Wesley's needlework case, John Wesley's spectacles and china: Wesley's Chapel, London. **8** West Street Chapel: *Wesley His Own Biographer.* **9** Foundery plaque: photo by Susan Pellowe. **18** Miss Sarah Wesley: detail from Claxton's *The Holy Triumph of John Wesley in His Dying*: Permission and photo courtesy of Methodist Church Overseas Division (Methodist Missionary Society), London. **21** Newbiggin Chapel: Geoffrey E. Milburn, photo by Harold Beadle. **23** John Wesley preaching in Gwennap pit, engraving: *Wesley His Own Biographer.* **24** St. Giles Cripplegate, old print, Author's Collection. **31** John Wesley by Thomas Horsley: Wesley's Chapel, London.

September
1 Ballad sheet: Wesley's Chapel, London. **2** Weardale Chapel: Geoffrey E. Milburn, photo by Harold Beadle. **3, 8** Susanna Wesley engraving by T.A.Dean, Wedgwood Wesley Teapot: Wesley's Chapel, London. **10** Stable Yard behind The New Room:Courtesy of John Wesley's Chapel, The New Room, Bristol; photo by Mark R. Wallis. **11** Boat in storm: *Wesley His Own Biographer*. **15** Plaque on Wesley home in Bristol: Courtesy of John Wesley's Chapel, The New Room, Bristol; photo by Mark R. Wallis. **18** John Wesley by Nathaniel Hone: By courtesy of the National Portrait Gallery, London. **19** Statue of John Wesley: photo by Mark Trewin. **24** Charles Wesley, Jr.: Author's Collection. **27** John Wesley engraving by Bromley and Susanna Wesley, the Lincolnshire portrait: Wesley's Chapel, London.

October
1 John Wesley's New House, City Road; photo by A.F. Kersting. **4** Epworth Kitchen, photo by Susan Pellowe. **8** Mary Vazeille (Mrs. John Wesley): Courtesy of Geoffrey E. Milburn. **11** St. Andrew's Parish Church interior, showing 19th century refurbishment in photo by E.W. Carter: The Wesley Historical Society Library, Oxford, England; Samuel Wesley, Jr., engraving: Reproduced from the collections of the Methodist Archives and Research Centre, the John Rylands University Library of Manchester; Embarkation from Gravesend: *Wesley His Own Biographer*. **13** Leviathan: *Dissertations on the Book of Job*. **16** Samuel Wesley, son of Charles Wesley: Courtesy of John Wesley's Chapel, The New Room, Bristol. **23** Frontispiece to *Maggots*: Wesley's Chapel, London. **30** Death mask of John Wesley: *Epworth to London with John Wesley*; photo by G.W.Edmondson 1890.

November
1 City Road Chapel engraving, *Wesley His Own Biographer*. **5** Memorial plaque on Charles and Sarah Wesley's home in Marylebone: photo by Mark Trewin. **9, 10** Fetter Lane Chapel and The Foundery: *Wesley His Own Biographer*. **12** Samuel and Susanna Wesley, drawing by Richard Douglas. **14** Wesley Street sign in Marylebone: photo by Mark Trewin. **15-16** Cartoon of Charles Wesley et al by Miss Sarah Wesley: Reproduced from the collections of the Methodist Archives and Research Centre, the John Rylands University Library of Manchester. **23** St. Andrew's Parish Church, Epworth, old engraving: The Wesley Historical Society Library, Oxford, England. **27** Quilt piece: Courtesy of Trustees of The Old Rectory.

December
1 Memorial to John and Charles Wesley in Westminster Abbey, an engraving: Courtesy of Richard Douglas. **8** Orphan House, Newcastle: The Wesley Historical Society Library, Oxford, England. **13** John Wesley's electricity machine at City Road: photo by A.F. Kersting. **17** John Westley, father of Samuel Wesley: Wesley's Chapel, London. **22** John Wesley engraving by William Hamilton: Courtesy of the National Portrait Gallery, London. **23** Charles Wesley statue at New Room, Bristol: Courtesy of John Wesley's Chapel, The New Room, Bristol; photo by Mark R. Wallis. **31** Epworth Rectory with Haycart: Courtesy of Richard Douglas.
Photo of editor on back page: David Renar.

Cover Design: David Renar, Renar Studios, Chicago.

A NOTE ON THE TEXT
Most quotations have come from printed sources in the public domain. However, specific thanks is due to the John Rylands University Library of Manchester for the privilege of researching original documents and for permission to quote from Wesley family letters and from Susanna's journal, particularly (all from Reference DDWF) Jan 2 (2/24) & 15 (2/23); Mar 30 (2/12); Apr 3 (2/22), 27 (2/26), 29 (5/12), & 30 (13/3); May 14 (2/21); June 16 (13/5); July 1 (2/16), 3 (5/8), 12 (12/9), 24 (21/19); Aug 4 (6/10) & 18 (14/72); Sept 15 (27/7); Oct 10 (2/23), 11 (2/2), & 15 (6/5); Dec 19 (2/22).

Susan Pellowe, a Lay Speaker in the United Methodist Church, is a performer, director, writer, and educator. Named after Susanna Wesley by her parents — her father was a Methodist minister and historian — she has toured the USA, Canada and Britain with her solo enactment of the Mother of Methodism, *O Susanna!* Under the title of *PRESENCE*, she brings to life Biblical characters and *Laughter under the Steeple.* Susan also conducts seminars on religion and the arts and is a playshop leader for the Fellowship of Merry Christians. With degrees in Speech and Theatre, for twelve years she was Associate Professor and Director of Theatre at a university. Her acting and directing credits make a long list and she has published on a wide range of subjects.